Published.

The Proven Path

From Blank Page

To Published Author

CHANDLER BOLT

ISBN-13: 978-1539412335

ISBN-10: 1539412334

DEDICATION

I would like to dedicate this book to the following people:

My parents

They always wanted something more than "getting by" for my brother and me. Using their experiences — triumphs and mistakes, beliefs handed down by their parents, as well as ideas of their own — they created a map to success. From the factory floor where they met, they have worked hard every day of their lives, pouring their lessons and aspirations into the minds of my brother & me. I'm grateful for everything they've taught me and continue to teach me.

My brother

As two very different people born a decade apart, Seth has taught me so much about life. He's been my biggest supporter and always makes me laugh while also challenging my views of what is possible.

Kendall

Lastly, I'd like to dedicate this book to my good friend Kendall, who passed away at the young age of 20 before getting the chance to live out his dream. Kendall's abrupt passing was by far the largest defining moment in my life. It was a moment that changed everything. It gave my life a purpose, a reason, a drive—to make this world a better place, beyond myself. It's my "why," and it drives me every single day to achieve my potential and make the world a better place. Love you Kendall!
Working hard to make you proud.

DOWNLOAD THE AUDIOBOOK FREE!

READ THIS FIRST

Just to say thanks for buying my book, I would like to give you the Audiobook version 100% FREE!

TO DOWNLOAD GO TO:

http://self-publishingschool.com/s/published/audiobook

SELF-PUBLISHING SCHOOL

NOW IT'S YOUR TURN

Discover the quickest way to become a bestselling author in 3 months.

Even if you're busy, bad at writing, or don't know where to start, you CAN write a bestseller and build your best life.

With tools and experience across a variety niches and professions, Self-Publishing School is the most efficient resource you need to take your book to the finish line!

DON'T WAIT

Watch this FREE VIDEO TRAINING SERIES now, and Say "YES" to becoming a bestseller:
http://self-publishingschool.com/free

CONTENTS

Section 3

PRE-LAUNCH

Section 4

LAUNCH WEEK

Chapter 1

SNOWBOARDING TO SEVEN FIGURES

We placed the cursor over the publish button, ready to hit "submit," with no real idea what we were doing.

My colleague, James, and I had just turned our short productivity guide into a book, and we were about to publish it.

We had been writing it to help people like us, young entrepreneurs, who needed to be more productive.

When we started our fun, little side project, two and a half months previously, we had very low expectations. We never thought we would find ourselves moments away from publishing an actual *book*.

We originally thought we would make a twenty-page PDF and give it away to people. No big deal. No risk. Now, a twenty-page PDF had morphed into a book, and we were about to publish on Amazon—who would have thought?

Click.

The book was published.

James and I exchanged glances. It was out of our hands now.

Some doubt and fear began to fill our minds. We had little knowledge about publishing a book, but we comforted ourselves knowing it was just an experiment. Again, no risk (especially since we had such low expectations).

We hoped it could help us make a little money and establish some credibility for ourselves . . . We hoped it could help people and save them from learning all the lessons in our book the hard way.

Most of all, we hoped people would actually like it.

Putting your first book out into the world kind of feels like standing up in front of a crowd with no clothes on. It's revealing, you feel vulnerable, and you really hope people will like what they see.

GOOD NEWS!
Fast-forward to the next week.

My plane landed, and my study abroad experience began in Austria. My last hurrah before leaving the title "college kid" behind. I could no longer be called a "college kid."

Shortly after my arrival, my snowboard was sliding over the fluffy, white snow in the Swiss Alps. Because what else does a snowboarding American do on his first day in Austria?

I'd spent the entire afternoon snowboarding with friends, laughing, and planning for the future. I let my book shift to the back of my mind.

Bing!

I received a notification from James—*The Productive Person* had hit #1 on Amazon in the "Time Management" category, topping David Allen's *Getting Things Done* (a.k.a. the "Productivity Bible").

I couldn't believe it.

Frantically, I checked Amazon to see the stats for myself. I had to see this.

James was right! And to top it all off, David Allen had even lowered his price from $8.99 to $3.29 (cheaper than our book) to try and reclaim the top spot.

This was HUGE. I couldn't have been happier.

It wasn't until later the next day that I got my big aha moment. I was sitting in the chairlift with a few new friends, riding back to the top of the Stubai Gletscher for another run. In European accented English, one friend asked, "Hey Chandler, what's this about you having a book?" (He had seen my celebration when I found out we'd hit number one.)

"Yeah, I just launched one last week," I responded.

"I hear it's doing well. That's so cool. I can't believe you wrote a book. Is it actually making any money?"

I thought for a few seconds, and then replied, "We put it out there, and it's doing really well. I just found out that while I was snowboarding with you guys all day yesterday, the book made over four hundred bucks."

Not only was he blown away, but so was I.

That's when it hit me . . . I had an earth-shattering realization. Just as those words to my friend came out of my mouth, my eyes were opened to the world of being an author—gaining freedom, making passive income, and doing work once, but getting paid for it forever.

It's one of those things that once you see it, you can never "unsee" it. I'd gotten a taste of what it was like to make money while snowboarding and having fun—and I loved it.

I had no idea the initial twenty-page PDF we'd written for our entrepreneur friends would eventually turn into a bestseller on Amazon.

Our book was downloaded 5,274 times in the first 3.5 days, and it brought in close to $7,000 within the first month. Not bad for a little "guide" we initially had no intention of selling . . .

I didn't know it at the time, but my life would never be the same again.

THE DECISION TO DROP OUT OF COLLEGE

When my plane landed back in the US, *The Productive Person* was still at the top of the charts, and my new business idea was slowly starting to form.

You probably think I'd be pretty happy with all that, huh?

<u>Wrong.</u>

Before leaving to go to Austria, I knew college was no longer the best use of my time. I had known I was going to drop out before I went (remember—it was my last hurrah as a "college kid"), and the trip just solidified the plan.

I was pretty nervous, but after getting the validation I needed from one of my mentors, I knew it was the right choice for me.

It was now time to put my plan into action.

And then I remembered . . .

I had to tell my mom and dad I was about to drop out of college (talk about scary)!

HOW THE DECISION WAS MADE

A young, naive version of myself sat in that first meeting with my college guidance counselor and declared, "Alright! I'm excited for this. I've been waiting a long time to learn how to run a business. I picked this school because you guys are known for having a great entrepreneurship program. Put me in every single business class you can. Let's do this!"

My enthusiasm was met with a blank stare.

I looked over at my mom, and the both of us were wondering what was up. For some reason, I had a feeling I was about to have a "come to Jesus" moment.

That's when the guidance counselor informed me, "Um . . . errr . . . yeah . . . well, you actually can't take any business classes your first semester. First you have to take algebra, chemistry, world history, and some other 'prerequisites.' "

The blank stare she'd originally given me was now being shot back at her from across the table.

"Excuse me? I'm not sure if you heard me correctly. I'm only interested in taking business classes. I don't care about anything else."

"Yeah, well, you have to take your 'pre-reqs' first," she maintained.

I was undeterred. I pressed on. "Okay, so assuming there's no way around that, I should probably be able to start taking business classes my second semester, right?"

Another blank stare.

"Well, kind of. But you don't get into your real business classes until junior year," she disclosed.

"Three years? Three years! Are you kidding me? That's insane. I came here to learn about business, and I'd like to do that ASAP."

Needless to say, I left that first meeting with my college "guidance" counselor frustrated. College wasn't off to a good start. The first of many signs that this whole college thing wasn't for me.

To make matters worse, after finally attending a few business classes, I realized I was learning how to run a business from professors who had never run businesses before . . . and that didn't make much sense to me.

I learn by doing, not by theory. Maybe you're the same way.

In the middle of a lesson I'd ask, "This is really awesome! I'm curious about how you're using this in your business?"

The most frequent response was, "Well, I actually don't have a business. I learned this from a textbook during my MBA."

Sigh . . .

While I was going back and forth between internships and class, I quickly found myself paying less and less attention to the lectures. The "traditional class setting" rapidly began to mean nothing to me.

After I completed an internship, I realized my personal goal was to learn, *not* earn a degree. I thought to myself, "Why are you wasting your time sitting through lectures when you could actually be out in the real world, running a real business? That's the way to learn!"

When I couldn't find a good answer to that question, I decided to drop out.

This was BY FAR one of the scariest decisions of my life. I had absolutely no clue what I was going to do. I knew I needed to give myself time to mull it over, so I chose to spend some time in Austria to make sure being a college dropout was really for me . . .

And it was.

After making the decision, I knew one thing: I wanted to be in charge of my life—make my own money, create things from thin air, and actually make a difference in the world. And I wanted it right away.

I wanted to help people, to speak, coach, and grow my own business.

But how the heck was I going to do that?

How was I even going to pay my bills?

MY BOOK GOT ME THROUGH

At this point in time, my new business (a productivity course for entrepreneurs) was really struggling to get off the ground, and I was watching my bank account spiral downward to zero.

As I began to question my decision to drop out of school, my little ebook continued to keep me afloat by paying the bills and keeping my head above water. That's when I discovered the MASSIVE opportunity that was sitting right in front of me.

A no-risk experiment taught me just how easy it was to make money off of a book: You can do work ONCE . . . and get paid for it FOREVER! I was practically tripping and falling into the discovery of a lifetime.

From there, I told myself, "I'm going to do it again. I'm going to write another book."

#1BOOK1LIFE

After dropping out of college, I moved to West Des Moines, Iowa, into a house full of other entrepreneurs.

That's when my brother, Seth, and I began preparing for the launching of a second book: *Breaking Out of A Broken System*.

We envisioned this book as something big, something that would make a difference. So we decided to give all of the proceeds from the book to charity.

We didn't have a ton of time—Seth was, and is, a full-time musician on the road with his Grammy-nominated band NEEDTOBREATHE, and I had my business to worry about—so we got together and wrote the new book in *one week* using a technique I'll lay out for you later in this book.

During this period, even though I was still growing my business, this book, a sideproject, took the majority of my time. Although my friends (and fellow entrepreneurs) didn't understand why I was spending all of my time on a book for charity when I clearly needed to make some money, they felt inspired by what I was doing.

I guess from the outside looking in, it didn't make much sense for me to be working on a charity project while my bank account was spiraling downward to zero, but it was important to me.

To try and explain it—the book meant a lot more to me than just making money. It meant saving people's lives and making a big impact on the world. Its slogan was "Buy one book, save one life" (#1book1life). For each book sold, the four-dollar profit was set aside to buy life-saving malaria medication for someone in Uganda.

We launched that book with tons of support. We created a hundred-person launch team (I'll tell you how to do that soon) and tried every strategy and marketing technique possible. We were going for maximum impact.

We achieved total market saturation for *Breaking Out of a Broken System* with appearances on radio shows and in newspapers, blog posts, and podcasts. We were everywhere, creating amazing publicity for the book and the cause.

It was during the launch of this book that I realized the power of books and how I could use the benefits I was reaping to help others launch their own books.

My first book was the birth of an entire business, but it was *Breaking Out of a Broken System* that showed me how big of a difference a book can make—and that I can make too.

These books put my new company and me on the map. I went from publishing a small PDF on Amazon to running a seven-figure business in less than two years.

All from one book, no risks, and low expectations.

LIFE TODAY

Fast-forward to April 27, 2015. As I was going through my morning routine and checking my email, I noticed an email from a reporter for *Business Insider*. They wanted to feature me!

As you can imagine, I was pretty excited.

As I was gathering my information, I realized the one common denominator for my rapid climb to the top of the online business world.

You might have guessed it: a book.

My entire business made $86K in revenue in 2014. Not a bad start for a college dropout, but, after expenses, it didn't pay the bills for my business partner and me. At the end of February 2015, when we launched another book, *Book Launch*, all of my bank accounts were negative.

Once *Book Launch* was published, our business BLEW UP. Within fifty-five days we brought in $92K in sales, from *Book Launch* alone, and our total business revenue reached $150K.

Book Launch cemented us as THE authority on the topic of writing and publishing your first book and brought in tons of business.

In my *Business Insider* feature, I boldly stated that our business, Self-Publishing School (SPS), was on track to hit one million dollars in 2015 (even though I had no idea how we'd hit it, and we weren't really "on track").

I'm a big fan of public accountability, so I knew it would force me to make it happen.

Book Launch and another book I released shortly after, *How to Not SUCK at Writing Your First Book*, helped me hit one million dollars before October, more than three months ahead of my "unrealistic" goal and less than nine months from the creation of SPS.

Today the business is on track to hit ten million dollars in 2016. And not only is it a successful growing business, but, more importantly—I am doing something I love and making the world a better place by changing people's lives.

Every step of the way, a book is what took me and the business to the next level, which was exactly the reason I wrote each one.

I shared some of my background with you to say one thing: My path to success started from one tiny ebook, and now I run a seven-figure business largely because of another tiny ebook. I know the best is yet to come.

In *Published.*, I am sharing my "secret sauce"—how to successfully write, market, and publish your first book in ninety days, an approach I called the "SPS 90-Day Way." I want you to reap the same kind of rewards that I've enjoyed. I want you to be able to leverage your first book to accomplish any future goals you desire, which, in turn, will transform your book into something much bigger than words on a page.

I want to give you easy access to that same accomplishment, freedom, and sense of worth. *Published.* is the map that will help you obtain any level of success you desire, even if it doesn't directly relate to writing a book. *Published.* is filled with tried and true, time-tested principles . . . NOT theory.

Since the launch of *The Productive Person*, I've self-published four additional books and helped thousands of people write, market, and publish their first books. So, the work has been done for you. All you have to do is read, pay attention, and take action.

The fundamental takeaway of *Published.* is for you to honestly believe you can write a book to achieve your dreams. If you honestly believe that and trust in the step-by-step approach I have created for writing, marketing, and publishing a book in ninety days (the SPS 90-Day Way), then there is nothing that can hold you back.

By following this advice, you will become a published author.

If this system worked for me, I know it will work for you too.

Let's get started by laying the foundation.

INSPIRATIONAL INTERLUDE

We all need inspiration, a bit of spark and flame to set us in motion, pulling our big "what-if" out of the clouds and setting it on the ground next to us, where we can see it as a real option and then choose to go for it. Commit.

I already told you that the primary intention of *Published.* is to give you such solid tools and so much motivation that you commit, with all your heart and mind, to write a book to achieve your dreams.

To help you along the way, at various points in this book, I am going to insert "Inspirational Interludes." These are true stories of ordinary people, just like you, who committed to the SPS 90-Day Way and wrote their first books. And, just as I promise will happen to you, this first book transformed their life. Just from that first book.

As you read each one, allow it to completely infuse you with inspiration, so you'll tip your scale to the side of—yes. *I'm going to do it too.*

FROM MEDS TO MOTIVATION

A book may not be a business, but you can easily make it into one, just like Michael Unks did.

Michael Unks, a pharmacist from South Carolina, attributes one teacher to helping him turn his life around. The teacher helped Michael become more confident in himself and develop a positive outlook on life.

Michael's powerful, personal transformation incredibly took place in only one month. Because it was such a radical shift in being, Michael felt compelled to write a book that could inspire family and friends to make similar positive changes in their lives too.

By following the SPS 90-Day Way that I'll be sharing with you in this book, Michael wrote and published his book *One-Month Willpower*, and enjoyed its rapid rise to best-seller status. Initially, Michael had thought maybe fifty people would read it. To his surprise, thousands of people are now reading his book. People are reaching out to him from all over the world saying how much the book has helped them.

One-Month Willpower gave Michael the confidence to keep writing, and to no longer look at it as a hobby, but as a new career.

Since then, Michael has written three more best-selling books, *An Rx to Get the Best from Life, One-Month Willpower*, and *Awesome in Hours*, and is putting the finishing touches on his fifth book. Michael is now pursuing a career in motivational speaking.

Michael's first book was the catalyst to creating a dream business: inspiring others to live better lives.

You can be just like Michael. He never thought he could build a business or brand from his books, but he did. Writing that first book was his ticket to believing in himself, and that was all it took.

If he can do it, so can you.

Section 1

LAYING THE FOUNDATION

Chapter 2

LOOKING FOR WHY

When it comes to writing, marketing, and publishing a book, the first step to take is discovering your purpose for beginning the journey in the first place.

When people come up to me and ask about writing a book, I ask questions to find their purpose: *What is your purpose? What are your objectives? Where do you want to go with this project?*

Whenever I am met with a blank stare or the answer, "Because I want to and it sounds fun," I look back at them and reply, "No, that's not good enough. Let me help you find the real reason why you are doing this, so it can help you later down the road."

Maybe you answered: it's a bucket list item, it will challenge me, or I want people to enjoy reading the book.

I'm sorry, but those answers aren't good enough either.

Why?

Because, yes, each of those responses are *reasons* why you would want to write a book, but they tell me nothing about the *purpose* behind your book, your *objectives*, or your *end goal*.

Throughout the SPS 90-Day Way, the purpose behind your book is the thing that's going to drive you all the way to the finish line. If you don't know where the finish line is, how do you expect to get there?

CHOOSE THE DESTINATION

Begin with the end in mind.

Using a common theme in the creative process, we are going to start at the end and work backwards, an approach some call "backwards design."

If you are taking the "become a published author" goal seriously, it's time to start thinking like an author. The first thing to do to get in the book-writing mindset is—determine the end goal for your book.

Think about it. What level of success do you want for yourself and your book?

Maybe you want to be an Amazon bestseller, get a thousand leads for your business, or sell six hundred copies of a book YOU published.

Figure out the end goal for your personal situation, and keep it in the front of your mind.

SEARCH FOR PURPOSE

> Instead of asking, "WHAT should we do to compete?" the questions must be asked, "WHY did we start doing WHAT we're doing in the first place, and WHAT can we do to bring our cause to life [. . .]?"
>
> Very few people or companies can clearly articulate WHY they do WHAT they do. By WHY I mean your purpose, cause or belief—WHY does your company exist? WHY do you get out of bed every morning? And WHY should anyone care?

—**Simon Sinek** in *Start with Why: How Great Leaders*
Inspire Everyone to Take Action

Simon Sinek, author and TED speaker, is a guru of the *"why."* He demands that for both businesses and individuals to achieve fulfillment and profit, the main issue is not what they do; it is *why* they do what they do. And naturally, Sinek's emphasis on the *why* is foundational in the successful writing, marketing, and publishing of your first book.

Next to your end goal, you must also clearly articulate and establish your *why*, your purpose for writing your book. It's these two factors that make up the foundation on which all else rests.

To determine your purpose, ask yourself:

Why did I set that end goal?
Why is that end goal important to me?

Once you have solid answers to these questions, you will then be ready to articulate your purpose for writing a book.

The purpose for your book could be anything from fulfilling a personal passion project, to growing your business, to becoming an authority figure in your field, to extending your network even further, or even telling a good story.

Whatever it is, it has to be something beyond making money or putting words on a page. If the primary motivator is to make money or to have written a book (as in, check that item off the life to-do list), you need stronger motivators.. Those weak motivators will not supply you with the discipline and drive you'll be relying on in the coming ninety days. Your purpose must be much larger than that for it to serve as your foundation.

THE FIVE WHYS

After years of helping authors write books, I've discovered that most people fall into at least one of five purposes for why they want to write their first book.

Each of these are strong, first-rate purposes for writing a book. They're purposes that will provide you with an unshakable foundation all the way through the SPS 90-Day Way.

Passion Project

Passion project books are written for selfless purposes. The writer of a passion project simply wants to share his or her knowledge, experience, and research about a certain issue because he or she truly wants to enlighten others about a cause or topic.

Passion driven people want to spread the word, create awareness, and, maybe in doing so, raise money for a charity.

Breaking Out of a Broken System's purpose was to raise money for charity. This was our passion project. My brother and I kept in mind our charity and its' mission when we were feeling overwhelmed, exhausted, or just plain discouraged over the course of the writing, marketing, and launching of the book.

Maybe you have a cause, or even a personal experience that directly relates to a cause, that you feel passionate about. Perhaps you've witnessed firsthand the dire conditions of people living without proper water sanitation, and you want to bring attention to the issue.

Imagine all the people you could help by sharing both your personal journey and all that research you did along the way. Gather your passion and use it as the foundation for your first book.

Passion is a great way to nourish a project. However, as with anything else, you need to be very specific about why you are so passionate and continue to set concrete goals, long- and short-term, for your project.

Money and Business Growth

As I mentioned before, I survived mainly from the proceeds from *The Productive Person* when I dropped out of college. We made close to $7,000 the first month and between two to four thousand dollars each month after. And our book continues to bring in money today.

Writing a book can be a great revenue generator. On top of that, it is the perfect way to capture leads if you are building a business.

Look at getting leads from your book as a long-term investment. Your readers have already bought one product from you. Now you have the opportunity to get them to buy another.

Plus, as I already wrote, if making money is the primary purpose behind writing your book, it means that from the start, you have a weak foundation. Don't expect to last the ninety days with money as your primary motivator. It just doesn't work.

Build Authority

When you're first starting on the journey to success, you have very little proof of how valuable your insights are. Sometimes having no reputation at all is just as hard on you as having a bad one.

If you want to gain credibility in your field or create credibility in a new field, a book is the perfect starting point. You can talk about how awesome you are until you're blue in the face, but without proof, your words are empty.

Plus, your book can serve as a kind of heavyweight champion business card. When you are meeting the movers and shakers whom you'd love to work with, you don't have to hand them a card that they'll easily toss away or lose in the mix of the many others.

Instead, you give them a copy of your book. Its physical presence will work as a stand-in for you because when they see it on their desk, in their bag, or on a shelf, they'll think of you. Your book serves as a reminder, propelling them to contact you.

After adding "author" to your resume, when talking to prospects, you can again use your book as a glorified business card.

Grow Your Network

A book is a great way to connect with influential people in your industry—such as other authors, journalists, podcasters, and bloggers—who can grow your network in some amazing ways.

There are always people in your field you can learn from. Having a best-selling book gives you the perfect reason to talk to the people you look up to. Maybe they will even reach out to you!

Being an author evens the playing field between you and them, making you respectable from the start.

Share Your Story

So many of us out there simply have stories to tell. Whether it's a biographically-based tale of triumph, a step-by-step guide to solving a problem, or a fictional story crafted to entertain (yes, that includes children's books)—they are all stories inside you waiting to get out.

No matter what your story is, you can use it to make a difference in the lives of the people who read it. You have all these wonderful ideas running wild in your head. It's not fair for you to keep something so great trapped inside.

Why not share it? You never know what impact you are going to have.

Regardless of what your purpose is behind writing a book, whether you choose one of the five reasons listed above or make your own hybrid, having a clear vision as to why you are doing the book will make your writing much clearer and detract from the possibility of your losing focus.

Your Turn—Fill in the Blank

End Goal: _The level of success I'm aiming to achieve with my first book is_

_____

_____

_____

Purpose: _My purpose for writing my first book is_

_____

_____

_____

BEST-SELLING AUTHOR TIP!

In big, bold letters, write the end goal of your book at the top of a sheet of paper. Under that, write the *purpose* for your book. Post this paper somewhere in your writing space where you can see it every day.

To make this even more official, I recommend signing a binding contract with yourself, stating that you will get your book finished, you will achieve your end goal, and you will not lose sight of the purpose you have set for your book.

You can download and print a copy of the "Contract with Myself" document we use at SPS here:

http://self-publishingschool.com/s/published/contract-to-myself

Once you have the contract, print and sign it, and set it up beside your end goal and purpose paper. Let these two papers guide your pursuit of the SPS 90-Day Way from start to finish.

Peter Soros, an experienced photographer, decided to turn his talents into a book in order to build more authority and grow his business. So, Peter signed the "Contract with Myself" and never allowed fear to hold him back again. After diligently pursuing the SPS 90-Day Way, Peter's book, *Photo Wow!*, is topping the best-selling charts in Amazon.

Just as Peter's purpose was the backbone of his success, your purpose will be the backbone of your success. A strong purpose paired with the "Contract with Myself" will allow nothing to stand in the way of your triumph!

So, take the time to find your purpose. And if you need extra help, that's fine. At Self-Publishing School, we provide our students with an entire Action Plan (or mini-course) just on finding your purpose. Go here http://self-publishingschool.com/s/ap-2 to find out more.

Yes, it is going to be an intense ninety days, following my step-by-step approach to write, market, and publish your first book. Yes, you'll have to shake up your regular routine to meet the big goal. Yes, you'll have to leave your comfort zone. But now you are equipped with two essentials—your particular end goal and your purpose, not to mention the "Contract with Myself." You'll return to these for clarity, grounding, and assurance, time and again in the weeks to come.

Before we address the practicalities, methods, and strategies that will aid you in the actual writing of your first book, as well as in the marketing and publishing of it, I want to supply you with one more essential piece of gear, one that you'll find yourself leaning on and digging into at critical junctures over the following weeks—the published author's mindset.

Chapter 3

THE PUBLISHED AUTHOR'S MINDSET

The published author's mindset is the final component in the oh-so crucial foundation you must establish before diving into the writing of your book. The published author's mindset involves (a) carefully considering the reality of publishing and (b) acknowledging that you may have some self-imposed limiting beliefs.

The first concern is publishing—traditional publishing vs. self-publishing. When Amazon came to life, they disrupted the publishing industry forever by giving authors a platform to self-publish their books, thus, giving them the freedom to flourish outside of the antiquated traditional publishing model.

Until recently, most people believed that getting published through Amazon was for authors who weren't really good at writing or for the rejects that couldn't get signed by a publisher.

But the truth of the matter is—many self-published authors choose to be self-published; they turn down publishing houses by choice.

The poster child for the self-publishing phenomena is Hal Elrod. Hal Elrod is a writer who pursued traditional channels (a big publisher) with his first book, which ended up doing fairly well.

Then, with his next book, *The Miracle Morning*, rather than continuing with the big publisher, he decided to self-publish and has achieved extreme levels of success. Specifically, his book brings in $20K-plus per month, just from Amazon revenue, and he's sold over 100,000 copies of his book. And I haven't even mentioned the speaking gigs, TV appearances, and radio and podcast interviews.

Hal's not the only one. Stephen King, Seth Godin, James Altucher, Tucker Max, and many other traditionally published authors have turned to self-publishing.

BIG PUBLISHING—EXPOSED

There are many reasons publishers are being put out of business and self-publishing is becoming the new norm.

Here are just a few reasons it doesn't make sense to publish traditionally:

- o It takes years to write and publish a book with a publisher
- o The publisher takes the lion's share of the book royalties
- o They do almost zero marketing for your book
- o You're stripped of most of your creative liberties (the publisher makes the final decision on what can and can't be in the book)
- o You lose the rights to your book
- o If you don't sell enough books, you're often required to payback your advance or buy back unsold copies of your book

On top of all this—it is nearly impossible to get signed with a publisher when getting started as a writer. They know you don't have the reach of an established author, so they see you as nothing more than lousy investments.

Even if your book is the best thing they have ever read.

These are just a few of the reasons that, now more than ever, it makes more sense to self-publish than to go through a traditional publisher.

THE TRUTH

Exposing all these truths about big publishing leads me to report one final truth about authors.

If aspiring authors were honest with themselves, they'd admit that wanting to get signed by a publisher has very little to do with the benefits from the publisher and a lot more to do with the validation that having a publishing deal provides.

By having a big name publisher back your book (and like it enough to do so), you get reassured that what you are doing is worthwhile. Some outside party is giving you a pat on the back, reassuring you that your message is unique and worthy enough for the publisher to put their name on it too—and that certainly feels great.

It's human nature. We all want recognition for our work. Yes, it feels good to have our parents, friends, and colleagues congratulate us and expound upon how meaningful, helpful, and brilliant our book is.

But what if I told you—so many more people are going to see your book and give you instant gratification and immediate validation for all your hard work when you self-publish your book?

Reviews of your work, messages to your book's Facebook page, and emails will come pouring in. Readers from all over the world will contact you with praise, questions, and stories of their own.

On top of all that, you'll be getting checks every month from your online book retailer after writing and publishing your book with complete freedom and control.

Joelle Casteix, author of *The Power of Responsibility* and already well rooted in big publishing, decided to try out the SPS 90-Day Way of writing, marketing, and launching a book to see how the results compared.

For her earlier books, Joelle invested thousands of dollars into a publicist and even got as far as landing spots on *MSNBC* and *CNN*, but her books still weren't selling.

"Traditional publishing is a long process," admits Joelle. "Plus, you don't really own anything, and you are still the one paying the bill. You can't change anything about the marketing of your book, even if it isn't working. Publishers don't get it, and they *don't* care."

In self-publishing *The Power of Responsibility*, Joelle shared, "The results I had with my latest book launch, using the SPS 90-Day Way, were amazing . . . I finally [had] the opportunity to become a 'real author.' "

Joelle's results truly are staggering. *The Power of Responsibility* is number one in five categories within Amazon.

Joelle is now selling roughly fifty books a day whereas previously, with traditional publishing, she was lucky to sell fifty copies in months.

The SPS 90-Day Way gave Joelle the ability to accomplish a lifetime dream. People who don't know her are buying her book every single day.

So, how are you going to be a successful, self-published author, like Joelle, and beat the publishing houses?

You are going to trust in the system I have laid out for you in this book.

EMPOWERING BELIEFS

Even though I could sit here all day and write about how great self-publishing is, that's only the first layer of the critical mindset you need to establish before jumping into the the prewriting and writing processes.

The second layer of the writer's mindset involves determining and then ridding yourself of any doubts and fears that may be polluting your mind.

All the thoughts and fears that are swirling through your head (or that eventually will be when you decide to write your book) are the same thoughts going through just about everyone's mind the first time they write a book.

If you let these limiting beliefs take charge, they'll win, and they'll convince you not to write the book.

However . . .

If you conquer them, the book-writing process becomes effortless.

Rather than wait to deal with these negative thoughts later on, let's address those limiting beliefs before you start writing.

Limiting Belief #1: The timing isn't right . . . yet.

This is my personal favorite. I talk to people all the time who want to write a book but "the timing just isn't right." They tell me they plan on writing a book "someday," maybe even "next year," when "the timing is right," as if the passing of time will magically free up their schedules.

What happens? Time passes, and they're just as busy, maybe even busier than ever.

As Zig Ziglar remarked, "If you wait for all the lights to turn green before starting your journey, you'll never leave your driveway."

To illustrate this point, I like to think of going on a family vacation. You get everyone in the car (for my family, it was an old, beat-up Suburban). You get the kids, the dog, the luggage, and you're all set to go.

You pull to the end of the driveway and announce:

Crazy, right?

You'd never leave the driveway.

As crazy as that sounds, this is exactly how most people view writing their first books.

Spoiler Alert
The timing will never be "just right." The stars will never align. You'll never be free from all responsibilities with nothing but time to work on your book.

You'll simply have to get started before you are one-hundred percent "ready." Even if you have children, two jobs, a busy schedule, and a business to run, no matter how much you prepare or how much time you have, you are never going to be completely "ready" for this.

As Napoleon Hill advised, "Do not wait; the time will never be 'just right'. Start where you stand, and work with whatever tools you may have at your command, and better tools will be found as you go along."

Limiting Belief #2: I'm worried the book will flop, and I will be embarrassed.
This is a huge limiting belief to get over, one that most people never conquer. You're thinking you will invest all your time on a book, and it might not be worth it. The book might fail, and everyone will know.

The process seems like a big time commitment for an unsure return. You have no confidence in your marketing ability. You may have no audience and no idea how to successfully build one.

It's *your* responsibility to wage war on these negative thoughts and turn them into positive ones, but it's *my* responsibility to give you the ammo you need to win the war.

Limiting Belief #3: I'm not an expert.
I've got good news: you don't have to be! With the rise of self-publishing,

people no longer care if you're published by a big-time publisher, if you have a PhD, or if you've won some fancy award. All they care about is what you have to say.

The most effective books are ones that give stories of transformation or personal experience:

o   Why you do what you do
o   How you've used your knowledge and skills to help others
o   How it made you and them feel
o   How you started from nothing and worked your way to the top

It's all about the packaging and the way you give information. The greater the personal touch, the more people will connect with your message.

Don't sell yourself short on the value of your personal story—it's much more powerful than you think.

Just because you're not an "expert," doesn't mean you won't help people with what you have to say.

As long as you provide value, people will enjoy your book; and you don't have to be an expert to add value. You don't even have to be a so-called "good writer."

Limiting Belief #4: I'm not a writer (I'm bad at it and/or don't like it).
I've heard this one from so many people: "But you don't understand! I'm not a writer. I hate writing."

I get it. I hated writing too. If you'd told me a few years ago that I'd go on to write multiple bestsellers, I would've laughed.

There's good news though: **it's called "best-selling author"** *not* **"best-writing author."**

That is one lesson, taught by Robert Kiyosaki in his book *Rich Dad, Poor Dad*, that I have carried with me from the time I first came across it in high school.

Kiyosaki explains, in multiple interviews, that you don't have to know how to write. You just have to know how to sell what you've written. That is what distinguishes the good books from the bad. You don't have to be a good writer to easily write a book and get your message out there.

A book is just a collection of personal stories and experiences. Inside you right now are dozens, maybe hundreds, of stories.

Instead of a *writer*, think of yourself as a *storyteller* . . . sharing your message and experience with people who desperately need to hear it.

Limiting Belief #5: I'm not tech-savvy, so I can't publish a book.
If you are one of the many "technologically challenged" people out there, PLEASE focus on what I'm about to tell you.

You do not need to be a tech genius or a social media savant to publish your first book successfully.

At least, not with the SPS 90-Day Way, that is.

Knowing a little bit about basic technology and social media won't hurt. However, if you were able to successfully purchase this book and read it this far, you have all the prerequisite skills necessary to write, market, and publish your first book.

The tech aspect of publishing a book isn't difficult.

Don't worry about messing something up with technology. Mistakes happen, and they can always be fixed. Plus, you will find some step-by-step handholding at many points in this book.

Limiting Belief #6: I don't have a book idea (or anything to say).
The fact is, there are already four to five books inside you right now. You have the knowledge for each of these books in your head already. You have many more life experiences and much more knowledge than you think. It's just buried over years of repetition and new life experiences.

A book can be written about anything: from the showing of farm animals at state fairs to investing in the stock market. Anything. The possibilities are endless.

So many times when I've taken people through the writing process, it has gone like this: they start without an idea, or maybe they have an idea but don't think it's enough for an entire book.

Then, they go through some foolproof pre-writing strategies (which I'm introducing to you in the next chapter), and after about fifteen minutes, they realize that they have SO MUCH to write about.

They come back to me very excited and declare, "Chandler! I didn't think I had enough to write a whole book, but now I have so much that I don't know how I'm going to fit it all in. I think I'm going to have to break it up into multiple books."

This happens almost every single time. And it'll happen to you too.

Limiting Belief #7: Books take a long time to write.
Let me just get this out of the way up front: books don't take a long time to write, so it doesn't matter if you're extremely busy.

I wrote my first book in a month and my second in a week. One was forty-five pages and the other 225.

Want to know something? The forty-five-page book outsold the 225-page book like crazy.

As you'll soon discover, I've simplified the writing process, so you can easily write your first book in thirty days, with approximately one hour per day blocked out for writing.

Don't think you have that much time?

Actually, you do. Just get off social media, push aside your favorite TV show, or stop playing those video games. All of these time-consuming activities will be there when you get back, but you'll never find a better time to pursue being an author.

Limiting Belief #8: My book needs to be perfect. (My first book is going to be my best book.)
This is what keeps so many people from trying to write a book in the first place. It keeps people sitting on a half-written book and editing it for years. They get sucked into the never-ending process of tweaking the same information over and over.

To solve this problem, I recommend following the old Facebook motto, "Done is better than perfect," because it couldn't be more spot-on.

Getting the first draft *done*, not perfect, is the most important thing to think about when writing your book.

Keep this in mind: you can always go back and tweak anything you write later because, believe it or not, after you release your book, it still isn't set in stone (another big perk in the modern era of self-publishing)!

With self-publishing, at any time you want, you can re-upload an updated version of your book. So, you can fix any mistakes as soon as they arise.

For this reason, it doesn't pay to sweat the small stuff, to stop writing until you land that so-called "perfect word." Your big aim is to finish your first draft. So keep that pen moving or those fingers typing away, whichever the case may be.

Limiting Belief #9: Writing fast = a low-quality book.
The speed in which you do something has little to do with the quality of work you produce.

To understand what I mean, consider Parkinson's Law, which states, "A task will swell in proportion to the amount of time you give yourself to complete it." Essentially if you give yourself a long time to complete a project, you'll actually give it less focus and it will drag on for longer than necessary.

Therefore, if you have a shorter deadline, you'll produce a much higher quality book in a more focused time period.

Instead of thinking that fast writing means bad writing, cement this thought into your mind: *writing fast means being more focused.*

Working in manic bursts followed by extended periods of no work will not yield results. It is not the approach I'm presenting here. We will be proceeding in focused, efficient, daily steps to guarantee that you reach the finish line with your book.

Limiting Belief #10: I don't have an agent or a publishing deal. *and*
Limiting Belief #11: I don't have enough money to publish a book myself.
Allow me to debunk these two beliefs with a single stroke of the keyboard. You don't need an agent, you don't need a publishing deal, and you don't need "enough money" to write, market, and publish your book in this glorious age of self-publishing.

A few years ago, these would have been legitimate concerns. However, in the same way Gutenberg's printing press made books available to millions of regular people and not just the elite few, computers and the Internet have made publishing and marketing available to us regular folk too.

As far as money goes, to self-publish your book at an online book retailer like Amazon, there is no fee at all. You pay nothing.

The only time you could spend some money in the SPS 90-Day Way comes after you've written the first draft of your book. You'll see that I recommend you pay an editor to work with you to revise your first draft. Then I recommend that you pay a graphic artist to create a high-quality book cover. These are the only two points in the process you'll want to spend money, and I'll show you how to get these services done on a budget.

Even then, you aren't required to hire outsiders. You can do it on your own, or ask a friend, if spending a small amount of money is an impossibility for you and is holding you back from launching your first book.

An agent, a publishing deal, and "enough money" are fallacies. They don't hold, not in today's day and age. With your brain, your discipline, your heart's desire, and my guidance, you have all that you need to write, market, and publish your first book in ninety days.

HOW A "C" WRITING STUDENT OVERCAME THE FEAR

You can imagine how funny and ironic it was when everyone started asking me, a college dropout who *hated* writing (just ask my high school English teachers), for advice about how to write, launch, and publish a book.

In fact, I didn't just hate writing—I hated writing with a *passion*. I got C's on all of my college papers, and for me, that was just fine.

My motto in college was: *Give me a test, give me an assignment, just don't give me a paper to write.*

When I dropped out of college, I hoped I would never have to write again. It was actually one of the perks of dropping out!

To my surprise, and initially by mistake, I eventually created a fail-safe and tested system for writing, launching, and publishing best-selling books: the SPS 90-Day Way. Who would have thought?

With this system, I began to love writing.

Weird, I know.

Through constant tweaking and testing, the system I created continued to provide better and better results for everyone who used it. The results were so impressive that I decided to take on a handful of people (forty-four, to be exact) and personally teach them the SPS 90-Day Way.

Because of the huge success of those forty-four people, this system eventually became an online training program I run today called Self-Publishing School (SPS). Through SPS, we've created tons of best-selling authors and have shown them how to use their books to massively change their lives, thus, providing them with freedom to choose their next moves, whatever those may be.

As I was coaching these forty-four people, I realized most of them got too deep in their heads and ended up doubting themselves before they even wrote their first words.

That's when I realized the importance of dismantling limiting beliefs. Many people waste years of their lives trying to get over the misconceptions given in this chapter.

If you never truly believe you can write a book, the sad truth is . . . you probably never will.

A 180

Determine the limiting belief that's been holding you back, and transform it from a limiting belief to an action pledge.

For instance, if you realize that you've been haunted by *I don't have a book idea (or anything to say)*, then turn it on its head—*I have a lot of life experiences that I can turn into books. I just need to figure out the one to start with.*

Decide the limiting belief that's been holding you back, reverse it into an action pledge, and post it where you can see it daily. Put it next to your end goal and purpose sign (from the previous chapter) to create an inspiring reminder.

Determine your end goal and purpose. That will allow you to freshen up your mind palace, making room for the published author's mindset.

You've laid a robust foundation that is ready to support you, motivate you, and give you a good kick in the pants when necessary during the ensuing journey. So let's hop to it—it's time to get the writing-party started!

INSPIRATIONAL INTERLUDE

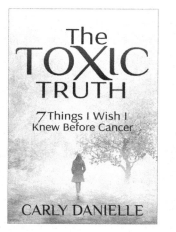

In a five-month time period, Carly Danielle's older sister and father were each diagnosed with cancer. Carly was devastated. But even more than that—she was angry. Her family had no history of cancer. Her sister was a health-conscious, active woman. Her father led a vigorous life too. Cancer just didn't make sense. Spurred by her sadness, a touch of anger, and great determination, Carly sought answers.

In her research, Carly learned that getting cancer isn't just due to genetics, diet, or activity levels. She found numerous articles by credible sources which explained that the liquids, solids, and gels that we expose our bodies to in our homes and at work are typically rife with carcinogenic chemicals because the FDA hasn't established firm rules in this area.

Carly knew she had to share this hidden truth with everyone she knew and beyond, and that's how she came to write *The Toxic Truth*. As Carly explains:

> The Toxic Truth is a passion project because it is my heart and soul. I do not hold anything back in my book. I put every detail out there for the entire world to read. Every chemotherapy treatment, every tear shed, every emotion I ever felt is in that book. It's not just my passion, it's my mission to tell the world this information because I was never told any of this and that infuriates me down to my core.

In her book, Carly not only educates readers about the reality behind popular household products, but also offers easy, cost effective alternatives:

> There is so much more than buying what's on sale or buying what everyone else does. There is so much more than what the "normal" tells you because "normal" is what got our society to this place where you know at least five people who have or have had cancer. That's not normal, that's wrong.

About the SPS 90-Day Way, Carly maintained, "[Chandler Bolt] states that you can write and publish a book in three months, and that is the truth. I was worried about making that timeframe true, and when I found out that he actually had a three-month timeline that told you what to do . . . it was a no-brainer."

Carly's passion for educating others about cancer and offering solutions has yielded amazing results. Carly is a #1 best-selling author in two categories. In the first two days of her launch, she sold over 1,400 copies of her book. And the hype is continuing:

> My life is straight out of a movie. Every regional newspaper is picking up my story. Every family, friend, or neighbor I've ever known is asking for a copy. People are even recognizing me at Target. All because I shared what I am so passionate about.

Chapter 4

WHAT TO WRITE

Kate Marie Pinkett, a writer from Texas, began her writing journey by struggling with what to write about. She had some ideas, but no standouts.

Initially, she wanted to write a book about how to be less angry. However, while implementing the brainstorming strategies you will learn in this chapter, she realized this book idea lacked focus for her.

After a successful meeting with her accountability partner (something you will learn about later), Kate realized her book idea would work better if she parsed it out over two separate books. As Kate advises:

> If you find yourself brainstorming, writing an outline, and feeling like the book really lacks focus or a specific central theme—definitely consider making it two or more! Better to have one really focused idea that you run with than making a long, convoluted [book].

Just like Kate, keep yourself open to options in this beginning, exploratory phase. Whether you have too many book ideas or one idea that just isn't working, these initial steps in the SPS 90-Day Way will allow you to discover a book idea that is the best-fit for you.

A WRITING RITUAL AND COMING UP WITH YOUR BOOK IDEA

Before you can start writing your book, you first need to figure out what you are going to write about.

I'm guessing if you bought this book and have determined your overall purpose, you already have a general idea in mind.

The following procedures are part of "pre-writing." They get your juices flowing and lay the framework for a successful book, whether you have a book idea or not.

The Free-Write Idea Dump

To begin producing sustainable book ideas, you'll want to use the free-writing brainstorming technique. This technique yields the greatest results and positions you to hit the ground running.

It's important to note: don't give yourself tunnel vision by only thinking about the initial topic you had in mind when you bought this book. You could very well be limiting yourself and not discovering what you need to write about.

Who knows—maybe after doing the free-writing exercise, you will discover a whole new book idea. I always recommend this exercise to my coaching clients, even if they think their ideas are spot-on and couldn't imagine writing about anything else.

When it is time for you to start free-writing, you will want to use pen and paper, writing by hand. I don't recommend jumping on a computer and typing it out. By actually forming the letters, you are using a different part of your brain and, in turn, allowing even more ideas to emerge and flow.

You will want to set aside fifteen minutes to write out book ideas. Keep your pen moving. Don't erase anything, just allow what wants to come out to flow freely; if nothing's coming out, just keep writing. Anything. Don't criticize and judge. Just go. Move the pen. The idea here is to keep writing for a solid fifteen minutes even if it means writing that you are tired and want to stop writing.

Start off by writing about your passions, interests, areas of expertise, and anything else that pops into your brain at that moment.

Feel free to write in single words or phrases, allowing your stream of consciousness to flow. Jot down ideas that energize you. Let them fall out of your mind and onto the paper.

Don't hold back.

Just get it out on paper.

The Familiar

If you are unsure of where to start with your free-write, keep in mind the purpose you already landed on. Also delve into the most familiar parts of your life.

Don't forget the familiar:

o *Your occupation*
   Maybe you have developed your own personal routines, rules, and perspectives about your particular work, things you didn't learn in college but only after years on the job. These are things that once you figured them out, you probably thought, "If I'd only realized this or done this when I first started! Then everything would've been so much easier!" Maybe new colleagues have sought you out, and this is the advice you've shared with them. In a book, you can help people gain your hard-won wisdom.

o *A hobby or interest*
   Whether it's an activity you regularly engage in or an interesting topic that you research on your own, you've probably acquired a lot of experience and knowledge about a particular subject that matters to you. You've already done the leg work, so it wouldn't be much of a stretch to package that knowledge into a book.

o *A passion*
   We all have issues and causes that really fire us up and get us talking. Often, these passions stem from a personal experience or the experience of a loved one, which then ties into an even greater cause. Health-, justice-, and education-related issues are universal causes that we each experience on personal levels.

o   *A learning experience*
    Many of us have made it through serious trials and tribulations—
    unexpected accidents; natural disasters; political unrest; grave
    medical issues; and physical, emotional, or cognitive challenges,
    to name a few. You have emerged on the other side profoundly
    changed with unexpected and clear insights. Numerous people
    would benefit from you sharing your experience and all you
    learned from it.

All of these potential book ideas give you the opportunity to add
immense value to a particular book niche and a particular audience of
readers.

No one has the same story you do, and it's time to use that to your
advantage. Take your job, hobby, interest, advice, passion, or intense
personal experience, and write it at the top of the page. Set a timer for
fifteen minutes, and begin free-writing on it. Chances are, if you can
(and want to) write on that one topic non-stop for fifteen minutes, you
know enough to write a book about it.

TOO MANY BOOK IDEAS?—HOW TO CHOOSE THE BOOK TO WRITE FIRST

While some of you might be struggling to craft your initial idea into
something that can become a book, I know there are others on the
opposite end of the spectrum. You have an endless amount of ideas
swirling around in your mind, and you can free-write about all of them.

While some would argue this is a good problem to have, for you, it
becomes difficult to decide which book to write first.

It's important to note that the decision needs to be made. You can't and
shouldn't write more than one book at a time.

If you are struggling with picking the first book you'll write about, use
these three criteria to help you decide:

What to do when you have too many book ideas.

(And how to choose the book to write first)

---

1. Which book could you write the fastest?

Hint: The idea you have the most material for and that will easily flow out of you

---

2. Which idea will most likely result in a finished book?

Hint: The idea you are most passionate about

---

3. Which idea makes you the happiest?

Hint: The most fun idea to write about, the most personally fulfilling

---

Go through these questions in this order. These questions are ranked in order of importance, so you'll want to rank the answer to #1 higher than #2, and #2 higher than #3.

If you have a book idea that passes all three questions with flying colors, that is definitely the first book you should write. If your book idea passes two out of three questions, that's okay too—get started writing that book.

If in doing the free-write idea dump you still don't land on the book idea that's right for you, do not stress out. Give it a day or two and perform the free-writing exercise again. Take heart that many first-time writers must revisit the free-write idea dump several times before the writing idea that truly resonates with them emerges.

For example, let's consider first-time writer Jody Coyody, a jack of many trades from North Carolina. Jody started her writing journey feeling "unworthy and abandonable." She practiced the free-write idea dump several times but didn't feel connected or sparked by what she was putting on paper. Finally, after much determination, she let go of her fears and allowed her paper to get messy and ugly. And in that chaos, she made two big discoveries.

First, Jody realized she'd been going about her pre-writing with the completely wrong mindset. Her problem was that before she even did the free-write idea dump, she'd already decided to write a self-help book because it seemed the easiest and most popular. However, she had no passion for writing "self-help."

Her second big discovery was that she figured out what she truly wanted to write her book about: certain, potentially controversial aspects about being a woman. This idea had actually been percolating inside her for about twenty-five years. It just took Jody a few run-throughs with free-writing for it to emerge clearly.

Just as Jody did, I encourage you to take every detail of these opening pre-writing stages to heart, even if they don't work out the first time. Start with a free-write that stems from your purpose and from the familiar parts of your life. Whether you are looking for an idea or have too many to choose from, I can't stress enough how important these opening, exploratory activities really are.

Once you determine your book idea, you'll be pretty excited. Don't waste that momentum; channel it to take your free-write to the next level—the mind map, which I'm blocking out for you in the next chapter.

Go team! You've got this. Let's move.

Chapter 5

THE MAGIC OF MIND MAPPING

As my high school English teachers and college professors (from my brief college experience) will attest, I was a "struggling" writer and a C-level English student.

While my friends could easily write five-page papers in an hour or two, I struggled more with writing: I would sit before the computer bewildered, then bored to tears, and then totally distracted. Maybe I'd manage a half-page. I would end up pulling an all-nighter to produce, if I was lucky, a C-level paper. I labeled myself a bad writer and knew writing was just something I didn't get.

So, later, when I knew I wanted to write a book, I figured I'd better get some help. I called my mentor, Adam Carroll, for some guidance, and while talking with him—*eureka!*—the epiphany occurred. Writing suddenly made sense.

On this call, he taught me about the magic of mindmapping, and how it makes the book writing process easy. That's what I'll be teaching you in this chapter.

BACK TO FOURTH GRADE

Remember bubble charts and tree graphs from elementary school? That's basically what we're going to do here.

I guarantee by the end of this chapter, or when you put the content of this chapter into action, you are going to have a giant—*eureka!*—epiphany too. After completing this exercise, you will realize you have way more to write about than you thought. And if you do it thoughtfully and earnestly, your book is basically going to write itself.

You already have all the knowledge buried deep inside your brain, as I said before. A mind map is going to help you tap into that knowledge and release it, so you can use it to successfully write your book.

Step 1: The Big Idea

First, get a blank piece of paper (preferably paper with no lines) and a pen to start your mind map. Once you have those, make sure you have access to a timer. You are going to need it.

In the center of the page, write your book idea. Don't worry about coming up with a book title or writing out something long. Just write a few words that represent your chosen topic.

Next, draw a big circle around your book idea and create lines jutting off of that circle. Right about now your image should be looking a lot like a drawing of the sun I did for my mom in preschool.

Now would be the time to get your timer out, set it for fifteen minutes, and hit "start."

Step 2: Keep Going

Out at the end of each of the jutting lines, you are going to write all the related ideas that enter your mind.

Think about the stories, examples, real-life experiences, and the book, blog, article, etc. you read that somehow relates to your main topic.

As you write your subtopics, they will likely stimulate more ideas. So you'll draw a circle around each of these subtopics, then draw jutting lines coming off of the subtopic circles, and record the ideas that stem from the subtopics.

You'll continue making more circles and jutting lines following the stemming subtopics as far as you can. In this way, you will keep building on your mind map for the entirety of the fifteen minutes. If you are still writing when the timer goes off, set it for another fifteen minutes. Don't limit yourself here. Tape more papers onto that original piece of paper if necessary.

It is crucial that you get your connected thoughts out on paper for as long as they are coming to your mind. In this way you thoroughly visit all the facets, subfacets, and sub-subfacets of your book idea in order to totally flesh it out. The more you can exhaust the possibilities in the mind mapping stage, the more efficient and fun the actual writing is going to be. So go for it!

Step 3: No Filter

The important thing with this exercise is to not filter anything. Just list out the ideas as they come to you. Get all your thoughts out on paper. Record all the ideas and race against the clock. This doesn't have to be organized, look pretty, or be "right." Do not censor yourself.

In fact, I've seen mind maps written on huge pieces of cardboard as big as a bed.

As you can see from the examples below, every mind map is as different as the person who created it:

Nothing is too crazy or too over-the-top. I promise.

The mind map will be messy—arrows, circles, lists, single phrases or words, misspellings, unfinished thoughts—it doesn't matter how it looks at this point. Get creative. Go deep into your brain bank, writing not only the obvious, but the potentially ridiculous and unfathomable too. The important thing is to just keep going until you cannot think of anything else.

> **IMPORTANT!**
> This is not an outline. We will get to that in the next chapter. You want to use this as an exercise to release your brain of all its ideas about the topic onto the paper.

THINKING ABOUT SKIPPING THIS STEP?

A mind map is a way to visually organize many ideas. It allows you to place idea after idea in a cohesive form that can eventually be structured into an outline.

Mind mapping is an elementary, yet important concept. People who fail at writing their first books often fail to take mind mapping seriously. That's their first mistake.

Mind mapping allows you to finish the writing of your book quickly and with minimal effort. Failing to mind map will lead to writer's block: sitting there staring at the blank page of a doc on your computer and wanting to bang your head against the desk because you don't know what to write.

Here is a picture from Jyotsna Ramachandran, a writer who followed the SPS 90-Day Way to successfully write, market, and launch her first book, Job Escape Plan.

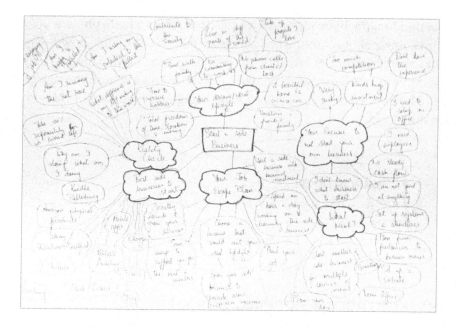

Like Jyotsna's, your mind map should get large and a bit unruly. That's supposed to happen. It's a good sign that you are turning those wheels in your brain to the point of exhaustion. It's in the next phase, when you create the outline for your book, that you bring order to those unruly ideas. In the next chapter, I'll show you how to set the outlining phase into motion.

Chapter 6

THE OUTLINE

Bringing Structure to the Magic

Now it's time to start transitioning into a part of the process that is going to play a huge role in finishing your book: turning your unorganized mind map into an easy-to-follow, structured outline.

YOUR MAP/GPS

Your outline is basically going to serve as a map (or GPS) to navigate your drive to a new place. When you drive to an unknown destination, you need directions telling you when to make turns, and where to go.

Your outline is going to supply you with the same direction and security. It will free you of worry and allow you to avoid a lot of wasted time. As with a map or GPS, your outline lays the writing path out in front for you to follow each day in the thirty days of writing.

Seeing the Forest for the Trees—and Analyzing It

When you complete your mindmap, you will have done a huge, somewhat connected, brain dump. There will be no filter: everything you think about concerning your book topic ends up on the page, no matter the relevance. Nothing is off limits; don't filter your thoughts at all.

When transitioning into the outlining stage, the very first thing you need to do is take a step back from the details of the mind map and look at the big picture. It's time to start looking at your mind map like a puzzle. Begin to ask yourself, "How can some of these bubbles fit together into one, cohesive puzzle?"

Once you start asking yourself that question, you will start to see how the bubbles fit together and how they can be grouped into bigger, umbrella categories.

Step 1: Find the Themes

Once you have taken a few minutes to step back and identify the common themes of the mind map, you are going to begin organizing the information in a more helpful way.

You should find at least three (and no more than seven) common themes. For clarity, I like to refer to these common themes as "sections." Once you identify them, these sections are what will compose your book.

From here, move to another large piece of blank paper and write your newly determined sections at the top of the page in big, bold letters. Each section name will act as the title of a column on this large piece of paper.

section 1	section 2	section 3
Positive Mindset	Powerful Mornings	Benefits/ Rewards/ Teachings

Step 2: Make a List of Ideas for Each Section

Under each of those sections, you are going to transfer the related information from your mind map to the new sheet of paper. In this way, you are making a list of the related, relevant information in the appropriate section column.

BEST-SELLING AUTHOR TIP!

Don't worry about making this perfect. Your sections should be quite rough at this point. That's okay. The clean-up will happen a bit later.

Unless something you wrote is very out of place and you know it can't be used, you should be transferring all of the information from your mind map to your new lists. And, of course, if you think of more related information at this point, be sure to record it too in the relevant section.

When my brother and I wrote *Breaking Out of a Broken System*, this is the exact method we used (as you'll notice in the following image).

By the time you are finished transferring everything in your mind map to your list, it should look something like this:

As you can see from this picture, all of our related information is organized into lists. You'll also notice that it is still very rough, but as I said before, that's expected. Also, it's okay if everything doesn't relate perfectly.

Actually, it's not supposed to yet.

Step 3: Finding Chapters

In this step, you are going to determine the chapters in your book. To do this, expect to do a lot of underlining, circling, drawing arrows (you can see all this in the images above and below), all for the sake of determining the leading ideas within each list (the "subsections" within each "section"). These leading ideas will work as your chapters.

section 1	section 2	section 3
Positive Mindset	Powerful Mornings	Benefits / Rewards / Teachings
- Counter every neg. thought with a positive one	- Gym	- How to's on section 1 topics
	- Healthy food	- Easy stress free life.
- Turn Your positive thoughts into action	- Water	More motivated
	- Run	More Success
- Surround Yourself with positive people	- Routine*	Life before/life after
	- Yoga	- More in line with Your life goals
-Influence	- Stress	
	- Coffee	↑
- Take control		Everything works together

Think of it like this—you have the **main message** of your book that can be summed up in a few broad **sections**. And each section supports a list of its own related ideas. From within this list, some of those ideas are predominant, leading ideas, called **subsections**, each of which also supports a particular set of ideas or **sub-points**. The *subsections* will be *chapters* in your book. The *sub-points* make up *content* that belongs in particular chapters.

I'm sure you can see at this point how crucial your outline will be once you start the actual writing of your book!

In the next step, you are going to take the lists one step further to complete the framework for your book.

Step 4: The Outline
Once you have the chapters identified, it will be time to move away from your big paper and back to the computer to create the outline.

You are going to take the lists and break them up into chapters (the-subsections). You should also order the chapters in a sequence that flows easily and makes sense for the book.

In a document on your computer, make a table in which you put every chapter in an ordered list, with the chapters correctly sequenced. Once your chapters are recorded in the correct sequence, add in all the subpoints (the content for each chapter) under their appropriate chapter headings.

Even at this point, you may suddenly develop more sup-points to add to a chapter. Go ahead and add them in too.

After you create those subpoints, begin to elaborate further on the subpoints as much as you can, going deeper and deeper into the content of your book.

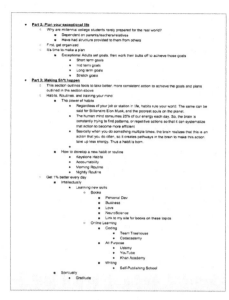

When you are finished, your book outline will officially be complete! And it should look a little something like this:

THE BEAUTY OF FRONT-LOADING

As any good writer will tell you, once you have successfully completed a thorough, organized book outline, your book will pretty much write itself.

Admittedly, when you actually take the time to make your outline, you'll find it challenging and time-consuming. It requires thoughtful, focused effort. But don't get discouraged. Putting in the hard work now will make the actual writing of your book so much more efficient.

Each day when you sit to write, you will have that roadmap right in front of you.

SOME CAUTIONARY ADVICE

Before you make your outline, I want to give you some words of caution based on my previous experiences.

A lot of my students either take following an outline to one extreme or the other—they either believe their outline is set in stone, so they must stick to it exactly or their book will be a flop; or when I advise them to view the outline as just an overall set of guidelines with the freedom to change it, then they don't take it seriously enough for it to be useful.

A FINE BALANCE
So what is the answer?
How should you regard your outline?

Think of the outline like a tight rope. It guides you from point A to point B, but in your walk along it, you are going to have to do some careful balancing. You'll have to make some small, back and forth adjustments to handle the rocky moments. It will certainly lead you to where you want to go, but you'll have to traverse it with consideration.

The purpose of this outline is not to figure out every single aspect of your book ahead of time. The purpose of the outline is to provide you with the path, the tightrope extending from starting point A (the opening of your book) to ending point B (the closing). The outline gives you lots of direction on your creative journey, but it doesn't determine every single moment of that journey.

MORE FINE BALANCING
Don't put too much pressure on yourself during this stage—but give your work some thought. Again, it's another fine balance. Yes, the quality of your outline affects the rest of your writing process, but understand that your outline isn't going to be perfect. You will likely move some things around, add and take away some topics, and change some aspects.

Equipped with your outline, plus a keen awareness of your end goal, purpose, and the published author's mindset, you will find yourself in the strongest position possible to get yourself on course and plugging away each and every day to get that draft written.

ONE FINAL PLEA
Before we wrap up pre-writing, I just want to give one final reminder to take every step of the pre-writing process seriously.

If you don't take the time to go through the steps we have covered so far, the writing process will be painful for you. The pre-writing processes I've shared will take a few hours to complete. And once you begin the writing of your actual book, you will thank yourself for having spent these few hours on front-end preparation.

At this point, with your invaluable outline in hand, you are ready to walk the tightrope, start the Thirty-Day Writing Challenge, and write the first draft of your book. We've arrived at a major juncture, and, from heeding my advice, I am one hundred percent convinced you are prepared. In the next chapter, I'll show you how to get started writing your book.

Chapter 7

THE 30-DAY WRITING CHALLENGE

Once you complete your outline, it's time to start writing your book. In this chapter, I'm going to show you how to get your book completely written, and written well, in thirty days' time.

Should you choose to rise to the occasion and attempt the Thirty-Day Writing Challenge, you will have to get a few things in order before you begin.

Once you have accepted the challenge, your singular goal is to get your rough draft finished. You should not focus on anything other than writing.

Below, I'm sharing with you the lengths of some books written by writers who employed my approach. Take note of the variation in the total number of words and chapters from book to book. While many of these books are between 15 and 30 thousand words (my recommendation), certainly not all of them are. Why? Because each writer has a unique message to deliver that required a particular amount of content.

Book Length Examples for Various Book Types

Passion Project **Books**

The Toxic Truth: 7 Things I Wish I Knew before Cancer by Carly Danielle	8,250 words 10 chapters
Live to Tell: A Suicide Survivor's Struggle with Depression and Anxiety by Ben Schwipps and Shelia Merkel	23,000 words 20 chapters

Grow Your Business Books

Get Your POWER On! A Savvy Woman's Guide to Becoming Confident, Capable and Compelling in Business, Life and Relationships by Nancy Jonker	31,000 words 9 chapters
Before You Swing: A Golfer's Guide to Fitness Training by Greg Justice and Derek Newman	20,300 words 8 chapters

Build Authority Books

Big Travel Small, Budget: How to Travel More, Spend Less, and See the World by Ryan Shauers	33,400 words 8 chapters
Such a Time: How to Live like Ester in a Rapunzel World: A Young Woman's Guide to Finding Herself, Fighting for Her Dreams, and Fulfilling Her Destiny by Samantha Roose	32,000 words 12 chapters

Grow Your Network Books

Super Spine Neck Check: Chronic Neck Pain Relief Once And For All by Sean Summer	18,000 words 17 chapters
The Career Upgrade Roadmap: 90 Days to a Better Job and a Better Life by Olivia Gamber	27,500 words 9 chapters

Tell Your Story Books

Nana's Shoes: A Story of a Family's Faith, Hope, and Courage in a Time of Ethnic Cleansing by Aisa Softic	77,500 words 10 chapters
From Farm to Market: Stories of Farmers and Artisans in the Carolina Piedmont by Lindy Mayberry Sellers	12,000 words 21 chapters

When coaching my students through the writing process, I have two rules:

— THE ONLY TWO WRITING RULES *EVER* —

1. You cannot edit while you write.
If you do, you will end up with three perfect chapters at the end of the thirty days and nothing more.

2. You cannot work on two books at one time.
You need to focus all of your energy into making one book great, especially since you are going to write it in thirty days.

From the time you complete your outline to the last minute you finish writing your rough draft, you are standing on very shaky ground. In my personal experience, I've discovered that these thirty days of actual writing are the most challenging part of the whole SPS 90-Day Way.

Even though you have a strong foundation to prepare you for writing, you'll still experience moments of discouragement and exhaustion along the way. When the negativity strikes, you'll want to lean on the foundational work we did at the beginning of this book for support.

Recall your purpose for writing the book when the hard times come, revisit the chapter on the published author's mindset to reground and re-energize, and lean into that outline you so carefully created.

STUDENT PAINTER SUMMER CHALLENGE —BIRTH OF THE 30-DAY WRITING CHALLENGE

The Thirty-Day Writing Challenge is no easy feat. You will be writing a book in thirty days! It's rigorous. It's demanding. And you'll feel like a million dollars when you achieve it. In a moment, I'm going to carefully explain it to you. But first, I want to share with you the experience from my life that gave me the idea for the Thirty-Day Writing Challenge—

During the few semesters I attended college, I participated in a special internship called Student Painters in which business majors learned about running their own businesses by hiring teams to paint people's houses.

During the orientation, I first asked, "What has your best guy ever done?"

I was met with a shocked expression and finally the answer, $130,000.

I, being my ambitious self, responded, "Okay, that sounds great. I want to do $130,000 in sales too, and I want to win *Entrepreneur of Year* as a rookie manager."

As you can imagine, my then-mentor, James Roper, told me I needed to pump the brakes a little. James did not want to set me up for failure. He wanted to set me up for success. Just like I want to do for you as you embark on your own thirty-day challenge.

After some back and forth conversation, James looked at me and asked, "Okay. You want to hit $130,000 in sales. What does that mean?"

So, we took my goal of $130,000 and broke it down into the average job size or how much money I would make for a single job. Then we worked backwards even further, incorporating statistics from previous Student Painter internships.

After some time and a lot of math, we ended up figuring out how many doors I was going to have to knock on each day to reach my end goal of $130,000. I even knew exactly how many flyers to put in mailboxes as I made my way around the neighborhoods. We got so specific with my overall goal so I knew exactly what I was going to have to do every single day to make it happen.

I applied a backwards design approach to figure out the daily and weekly targets that I'd have to achieve in order to reach my end goal in the designated time period. I used these results to create an overall "outline" of the work I would need to do.

My mentor, James, knew that lots of encouragement, a positive attitude, and hard work were not enough to help me achieve my end goal and purpose. He knew we had to make a deliberate plan based on realistic numbers so that the positive attitudes and hard work of my team and me wouldn't be wasted. We would be decisive and intentional from the start.

This exactly matches my approach for you—a deliberate and realistic plan for writing your book so that you write decisively and intentionally in the thirty-day time period and achieve your final goal: a draft of your first book.

THE THIRTY-DAY WRITING CHALLENGE—A COMPLETE DESCRIPTION

You should know me well enough by now to know I wouldn't challenge you to write your book in thirty days without showing you exactly how to break down your writing goals into smaller, manageable goals that will ensure your success.

Just like James was careful to set me up for success in Student Painters, I am doing the same for you here. I'll show you how to make a plan to successfully complete the challenge, so all you'll have to do is implement it to reach your end goal.

Following my lead with the Student Painters story, we are going to start with the end goal, work backwards, and come out with a strategy to help you successfully complete this thirty-day challenge!

1—Determine Your End Goal
Let's revisit a quote from earlier in this book. It is the second habit of "highly effective people" from Stephen Covey's *Seven Habits of Highly Effective People*: "Begin with the end in mind." This perfectly applies to you at this point in the journey.

Before you can do anything else, you have to determine the end goal for the Thirty-Day Writing Challenge: to finish your first draft. More precisely, your end goal is going to be completing all the chapters you have established in your outline.

2—Break Down the Goal
Let's say you are going to write a fifteen-chapter book in thirty days, just as an example.

The next step would be to break down that big end goal into smaller, daily goals. You should ask yourself, "What am I going to have to do each day to reach my end goal in thirty days?"

Your answer should look like this:

> If I am going to write a fifteen-chapter book in thirty days, then I'm going to have to write one chapter every two days.

Knowing how many chapters you need to write every day provides a daily indicator, telling you if you are going to reach your end goal, or not. Every day you must strive to meet the daily goal, thus, chipping away at your end goal, one piece at a time.

3—Expand Your Goal

In the second step, you determined the daily goal you must meet in order to achieve the overall thirty-day goal. In this third step, expanding upon the daily goals, you need to determine the three weekly goals you must meet to achieve the big thirty-day goal. At the end of week one, where must you be? Week two? Week three?

These weekly goals will serve as "mile markers" or checkpoints. They will let you know if you are on track to hit your big goal or if you are going to have to pick up the pace in the following week to get back on track.

Continuing with the example of the fifteen-chapter book and expanding upon the daily goal of a half chapter a day, you must complete 3.5 chapters per week.

THE DAILY SCHEDULE

Once you know how much you are going to have to write every day to successfully complete the challenge, it's time to drill down into what your daily writing routine should look like.

Chapter Mind Map: Each day you write a new chapter, you will need to do a bit of pre-writing on a much smaller scale. Before you write each chapter, you are going to mind map on only that specific chapter.

I want you to write the chapter topic in the center of the page with lines jutting off it. Then begin to record branching ideas and so on. Write everything you can think of regarding that single chapter, even repeating sub-points you've already recorded on the outline.

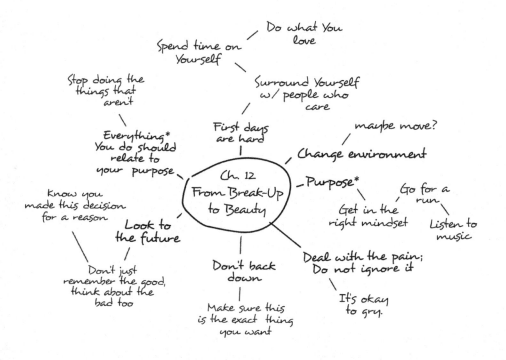

You should spend no more than fifteen minutes on this mind map.

Fine-tune the Chapter Outline: Then, once your chapter mind map is complete, you are going to add any of the newly discovered information on that topic to your existing outline.

Write: Using your outline as the invaluable map that it is, you'll set your timer, anywhere from thirty-five to ninety minutes, and write for the designated amount of time. You've already determined and sequenced the content you are going to be writing, so the actual writing won't be mysterious. It's simply a matter of doing it. And keeping in mind "The Only Two Writing Rules *Ever*."

Your daily time stamps should look like this:

Mind Map:	**Outline:**	**Write:**
15 minutes	10 minutes	35–90 minutes

With this schedule, you'll easily be able to get your rough draft completed in thirty days or less.

WARNING! Title-Related Rabbit Hole Ahead. Please Avoid! Because some of my writers have made this mistake, I'll address this common misconception up front: You do not need a title to write a book.
You only need a book topic.

Whatever you do, don't come up with a title before you are a hundred percent done with your manuscript. Otherwise, you'll end up catering your writing to that preconceived title, filtering what you write by whether or not it fits with the title you've already come up with. You'll write yourself into a corner that you won't be able to get out of.

Wait until you are finished writing your manuscript to come up with a title. This will give you the ability to write freely, without worrying about the title as you go.

So at this stage, you are using your outline, which is based on your book idea, to guide your writing. That outline should be so solid that it provides more than enough support.

TWO HEADS ARE BETTER THAN ONE

When you are in the trenches of writing your book, it's going to get tough. It will push you to your mental and physical limits. Some days it will seem easier to give up than to push through. That's why only the truly dedicated complete the challenge and write their first draft in thirty days' time.

Jyotsna Ramachandran

•••••••••••••••"Why is SPS worth 100 times its price"•••••••••••••••
I was able to get connected with my accountabilibuddy Stephen Parr from New Zealand because of SPS. We've been co-coaching each other for many months now and have benefited tremendously. Long after our books got published, we still continue to discuss various subjects related to our careers and life. It was a great experience to finally meet Stephen and his wife in person. They both planned a holiday to India and flew all the way from NZ and spent quality time with me and my family last week 😊
Takeaway message: Building lasting relationships with the incredible people you meet at SPS will make this course truly priceless 😊

While writing for thirty days is your responsibility, it doesn't mean you have to do it alone. One of the major keys to success as a first-time author is having an accountability partner, otherwise known as "private accountability."

Accountability plays a great part both in my business and my personal life. It plays a major role in my success, and I also see it play a major role in the success of all my students, just like it did for Jyotsna and Stephen:

I highly recommend you establish some kind of system of accountability when you begin writing your book. The best way to establish accountability is to work alongside someone else who is undertaking the same challenge as you and openly exchange your daily goals and progress with this person. And as you can see from the picture above, the relationship can last a lifetime.

No, your accountability partner is not physically next to you writing his or her first book; they may be from a different part of the world, just like Jyotsna (India) and Stephen (New Zealand). The point is that you two hold one another accountable to the writing. Not only can you keep each other accountable, but you can share best practices, failures, and anything else to help the both of you become more successful.

Follow this three-step strategy to help ensure you are held accountable for your work as a writer:

1. Find one person who will agree to be your **"accountabilibuddy."** Ideally this person is writing a book too, but even if he or she isn't, he or she can still hold you accountable to your goals. This person should ask you specifically about your progress on your book.

2. Make a **weekly commitment** to talk with your accountabilibuddy. Be prepared to share your wins for the week as well as anything you might be struggling to accomplish.

3. **Make your deadline goals public.** Share with anyone and everyone when your book will launch, how much progress you've made so far, and your weekly writing goals. Share your goals and progress with as many people as possible so that there are many people supporting you and also keeping you in check! Plus, as I'll explain to you later on, this is also a way to build buzz for your book.

You might feel uncomfortable sharing your struggles, but it's very helpful to share conflicts and losses with your accountabilibuddy, not just wins. Your accountabilibuddy may have a practical solution to your trouble or simply be a great listener.

It's also great when your accountabilibuddy shares what didn't go so well for him or her. You hear his or her failures and think, "Oh, wow, I'm not the only one struggling here. I'm not the only one feeling discouraged or embarrassed. There are other people in the same boat." In uniting with someone else and sharing your struggles, you'll end up realizing your power to overcome them.

Don't try to go through this process alone. Find someone that you know will be real and honest with you, even when it hurts. Know he or she has your best interests in mind and just wants you to come out on top.

Recall that with Student Painters, I only reached my goal of winning *Entrepreneur of the Year* because I didn't try to do it alone. Not only did I have great accountability with my mentor, but he also served as a coach, guiding me through everything I needed to do to reach my goal.

Having an accountability partner was great for me and will be great for you too. Take some time to find a strong accountability partner that will support you when you need it.

THE CIRCLE OF WRITING LIFE

Writing a book in thirty days is a lot like long-distance running, especially when you aren't in the best shape.

When first starting to train for long runs, you start small: setting short, distinct goals for yourself, like running to the end of the road, a trash can, or a light pole, and then allowing yourself to walk or take a break. You reach a certain point, you stop running and walk for a bit, and then start running again. This way you eventually reach your goal without overexerting yourself.

That's the same way your thirty-day writing will work. You've set short, distinct goals, one chapter or half a chapter per session, and that is all you need to worry about. As long as you stick to the plan, there is no need to worry about what you are doing as a whole. Before you know it, your rough draft will be finished, and you will see the light at the end of the tunnel.

I know this chapter is a lot of information that requires a lot of exertion on your part. However, when you implement it, you will be following it over a month's time.

What everything in this chapter boils down to is one simple, recurring cycle.

It's a circle, with each aspect feeding into the next and each part being equally important.

If you think about it, it looks like this:

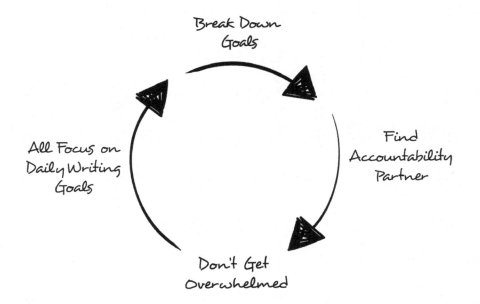

THE 30-DAY WRITING CHALLENGE WALL OF FAME

Because I know how hard it is to write your book in thirty days, when it's over, it's a time for celebration. And I want to help you celebrate!

When the time comes and you finish your book in thirty days, I seriously want to know about it. So, please join me in celebrating your success by posting a picture of you and your completed draft on Instagram, Twitter, or Facebook, using the hashtag: #SPS30daychallenge.

And after you've celebrated your completion of the first draft, you'll begin the fine-tuning. In the next chapter, I'll teach you how to self-edit and how to find, hire, and work with a good editor. You've already made the cake, your first draft, so let's put some icing on it, editing, to make it even tastier!

INSPIRATIONAL INTERLUDE

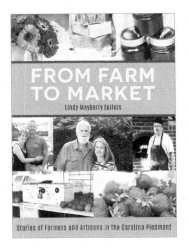

Stories of Farmers and Artisans in the Carolina Piedmont

In *From Farm to Market*, Lindy Mayberry Sellers shares the life stories of small farmers and local artisans in the Carolina Piedmont region. As Lindy explains, "Everyone has a story to tell, and since I have heard some fascinating stories from farmers and artisans that I have gotten to know through my time working alongside them at farmers markets, I wanted to be the one to tell their story."

She also felt motivated to write *From Farm to Market* "to inspire others to be innovative and have fun growing or making things to sell at the farmers markets in their area."

Lindy admits that her pursuit of the SPS 90-Day Way was not a breeze. For Lindy, the most challenging part was the book launch: "As the date of my official launch approached, I grew a little apprehensive and worried that I wouldn't have the time to devote to it or that I wouldn't 'do it right.'" So how did she handle it? She voiced her concerns to her community of supporters, who, in response, rallied behind her with encouragement.

With the supportive nudge of her community and the clear launch strategy steps laid out before her, Lindy's book soared high, spending two weeks at #1 in the Kindle "Green Business" category.

Even more important to Lindy is the local support she's received since publishing her book:

> I have a print book as well as a Kindle version. I have been pleasantly surprised at how well received it has been, especially within our community. When I first wrote the book, I said to myself, "I don't care if I sell any; I just want to let the voices of these wonderful people be heard." Well, their voices were heard because I have sold quite a lot of those little pink books!
>
> My high school English teacher [even] asked me if I would come and speak to her creative writing class on the process that I went through from writing to publishing. I have done five book signings and several interviews with newspapers in town. [My book] has given me credibility and has enabled me to sell more products at our local farmers markets—handcrafted soaps, jams, jellies, relishes, and bread.
>
> I had the opportunity to give a hardbound copy to our local library. That was possibly the best moment. The library has always been one of my favorite places in the world, and I have been going since I was five, when my father first took me. To see an actual book with MY name on it on the library shelf is huge.

I agree with you, Lindy: it is a huge honor, and one that you earned.

It's not a miracle that Lindy wrote, marketed, and published a book that reached best-seller status and has afforded her special recognition in her community. How she managed it is no secret. I'm sharing the very same path to success that Lindy and others have traveled.

It's Lindy's follow-through on her commitment to the SPS 90-Day Way that is remarkable.

You too can be remarkable. I'm giving you the path. You just need to commit to walking it.

Section 2

TAKING THE DRAFT TO THE NEXT LEVEL

Chapter 8

CRISIS OF MEANING

Finishing the rough draft of your book and then starting the revising stage is a lot like finishing an extremely hard day at the gym. You're ecstatic it's over, but you can already tell you are going to be pretty sore. Once morning comes, you're so sore that you have to give yourself a pep talk just to get out of bed.

Once you get out of bed, a realization hits you like a ton of bricks: it's time to head back to the gym and get ready for another tough day of working out. This is the point where you have your first crisis of meaning.

Starting the revision process is a lot like this workout scenario. You finished your super hard workout (writing the rough draft), and the last thing you want to do is repeat it (revising the rough draft).

But the funny thing about working out is, if you head back to the gym and work the soreness out of your muscles, you will feel stronger and pain-free quicker than if you had laid around the house and done nothing.

You will feel weary and reluctant to return to the manuscript, but proceeding with the revising will give you tremendous overall gains, whereas neglecting to revise will simply increase your weariness and reluctance.

In the "crisis of meaning" part of the book writing process, you will have reached the point where authors are separated from wannabe authors.

When you get to this point, it will be time to metaphorically head back to the gym and get back into the swing of things, even though your body and mind will want to resist.

To do this in real life, you are going to get your rough draft out, open it to the very first page, and begin the verbal read-through . . .

THE VERBAL READ-THROUGH

My favorite way of doing a self-edit process is to do a "verbal read-through." This means reading the draft of the book out loud to yourself and making changes in the manuscript as you go along.

When you read your own writing out loud, you can hear what the book will sound like in your target audience's mind. You transition out of your own head and into your reader's. Errors in your manuscript become obvious, as well as holes in your arguments and stories.

You can be sure you'll find spelling errors, grammatical follies, and punctuation mishaps. If you followed the first rule of "The Only Two Writing Rules *Ever*" and didn't edit as you wrote, don't be discouraged by how many errors you find during the self-edit. Instead, *be proud*.

No matter what, have fun with this verbal read through because once you are finished, the book will go to an editor.

HOW THE CREATIVE PROCESS WORKS

As noted already, after self-editing, you'll be handing the manuscript over to an editor, who is likely to be the first outside person to encounter your book in its entirety. While I'm sure you're excited and a little nervous to receive support from a professional, I want to acknowledge something in advance: the verbal read-through will likely be discouraging for you.

As I said before, I want to set this expectation from the outset: you are going to find a TON of mistakes in your book that you didn't know were there, and that's perfectly okay. No one has written the perfect book the first time around. Most first drafts need a truckload of work before they can be published. And that's okay.

As you enter the stage of revision and begin your verbal read-through, you'll be in the trenches of the creative process.

Which can basically be summed up like this:

1) This is going to be awesome!

2) This is hard.

3) This is terrible.

4) I'm terrible.

5) Hey, not bad.

6) That was awesome!

Yes, you might feel terrible about your draft the first time you read it, but look ahead. Keep your head up and revisit your end goal and purpose. By this point, you'll have already done the most tedious, laborious part of the process: writing the first draft. So now is the time for you to push through and trust that the best is yet to come.

STICK TO THE DEADLINE

I can't stress this enough: don't continue to revise your book forever. Don't be the kind of writer who revises for eternity, or you'll manage a few supposedly perfect chapters and nothing more.

This is one of the biggest mistakes writers make, and it's a detrimental one.

They never stop self-editing their books, so their books never get published. This is why you, your accountability partner, and/or writing coach need to set strict, hard deadlines for finishing the verbal read-through.

If you find yourself swaying towards revising your book forever, a good principle to return to is Parkinson's Law.

If you have a shorter deadline, you'll produce a much higher quality book in a more focused time period.

And don't forget, "Done is better than perfect."

It's better to have a complete, imperfect book than a "perfect" section of an incomplete book.

Once you have read through your book *out loud* at least one time, it will be officially time to pass the draft off to an editor and let him work some editing magic!

Chapter 9

WORKING WITH AN EDITOR

Passing your book off to an editor after you've read it through will feel like an intimidating ordeal. I know, I've been there. Many people feel like their work isn't ready for an editor's eyes, so they hesitate to pass it off, especially after having experienced a dispiriting verbal read-through.

Lotchie Burton received her first round of edits from her editor, and as expected, it wasn't a pretty sight. According to her editor, the book needed "extensive rewrites." Lotchie had to take a moment to accept that there was a lot of work ahead. But she also worried that she had written a really terrible book.

Thankfully, the editor assured Lotchie that the book was good, but it could be even better. The editor admitted to being tough, and it's toughness that turns good into great.

"My feelings were a bit bruised," admitted Lotchie, "but I wasn't about to disregard everything [the editor] said. I knew there would be some things I wouldn't agree with, but I also knew there would be things that made perfect sense. Although I was certainly disappointed in the initial assessment, I remained open-minded to recommendations and room for improvement, and moved forward from there. It was going to take a little longer to get to my final destination, but I was a lot further ahead than I'd been two months previously."

So, don't let bad news from an editor sway you from your purpose. Lotchie didn't, and you shouldn't either.

When you pass your book off to someone with a fresh set of eyes, you are giving your book a chance to reach a level that you can't achieve on your own.

THE UGLY TRUTH

Writing a book feels like a private act, and you'll likely worry about others' opinions. Not to mention, the editor you hire will probably be the first person to see your finished manuscript.

As a word of warning, I see more writers stall out and quit in the editing phase than at any other stage of this process. The writers continue editing for months, and their books never see the light of day.

And I don't want that to be you.

If you find yourself falling into this trap, let me just be the one to tell you . . .

You'll need to get over it. You just have to jump in with both feet and get the show on the road.

For example, here's what first-time writer, Margaret Skeel of Australia, noted about herself at this point:

> **Finished!** I've been dithering around in [self-editing] for way too long, but today I bit the bullet and said to myself with teeth clenched: done is better than perfect. I read through my book and it's OK. I have [just] sent it off to my editor for the final checkup.

Notice how Margaret had to force herself out of a stall at this point. Good job to her, and let this be a lesson to you too.

TICK-TOCK

If you and your editor work on your book for more than 3.5 weeks, you're just stalling and, therefore, wasting time.

Never forget, you are working with an editor to make the book better, not to make the book perfect. There is no such thing as a perfect book anyway.

You might think 3.5 weeks of editing is too fast, but it's actually just the right amount of time to get what you need done, if you are focused. It will help you get your book to where it needs to be without editing into eternity and wasting precious time and money.

When it comes time, buckle down alongside your editor in order to get your book edited in 3.5 weeks or less, so you will be ready to publish sooner rather than later.

In order to hit the 3.5-week deadline for editing, the process should look like this:

Day 1–2: Hire the editor and get him or her started.

Day 3–10: Editor does first content edit.

Day 11–16: You make content changes.

Day 17–19: Editor does final content edit/beginning copy edit.

Day 20–22: You approve changes and make final tweaks.

Day 23–25: Editor does final read-through and copy edit.

As you see here, you and your editor will pass your manuscript back and forth at most three times, which is all you need to make your book a success.

HOW TO FIND A GOOD EDITOR

Finding a competent editor for an affordable price is a lot easier than you may think. There are several straightforward ways to hire an editor, but there is one way I always recommend—turning to sites like Upwork or Guru.

Basically, you post a description of the project on a site like Upwork or Guru, and freelance editors from the site will make bids to work with you. What's great is that you can read the freelancers' profiles, browse their portfolios, and, most importantly, read client reviews to help you decide the editor whom you will hire.

When looking for an editor on Upwork or Guru, chances are a few will stick out to you, the ones that have good reviews or high ratings.

As you start to narrow your choices, you want to make sure you choose an editor that has a strong passion for what he or she does, not just someone who has good credentials and a fancy resume.

So don't always go with the editor that looks the best on paper. Go with the editor that will put in the work necessary to give you a final, polished draft. A great way to determine this is once you've picked your top choices, ask them to do a short sample edit (about three pages) to compare and contrast their work.

ON FEES

You may set your job up as an "hourly wage" or a "fixed-price" project. I recommend going with fixed price because this will really motivate your editor (and you too!) to get the job done in the designated timeframe. You can calculate the general fee you are willing to pay by multiplying the total number of words in your manuscript by $0.005 to $0.015. For example, if your book is 22,000 words total, then expect to pay roughly between $110 and $220 for the editing.

Certainly take into account the fees the freelancers are proposing, but don't make cost the single determining factor in whom you hire. The quality of work and your rapport with the person, even in your initial interactions (before you've decided on the hire), are very important too.

GOLDEN TICKET TEMPLATE

To help you zero in on quality editors, below is the posting template I use for all my editing jobs. I highly recommend you use this template because it includes a due date to keep the editor (and you) on track. If the editor knows your timeline before submitting a proposal, you have less to worry about later.

Also, this template includes a specific description of your book, so the editor will know what the job entails before bidding on it.

If you look closely in the template below, you will see that the freelancers are to include the phrase "purple cow" in their responses. This little addition ensures that you automatically screen out people who are responding to any proposal they see without carefully considering them. This will let you know who took the time to read your request.

Example Upwork Posting Template

I'm looking for someone with excellent English and literary skills to edit the content and copy edit my book.

The book has already been through a couple self-editing phases, but this is the final edit before the book will be published on Amazon in a few weeks.

It is a .... book that talks about ....
....

As far as the editing goes, I'm on a pretty short deadline, so I need someone who can work quickly and focus attention on this project over the next 3 weeks.

I need the content and copy edits completed by ....
(insert date 3 weeks out from expected start date).

The book is .... words, ... chapters, and .... pages.

I'm looking for someone with editing experience and with interest in this type of book.

Please be prepared to do a short sample edit (about 3 pages) too.

I'm working on this book with previous bestsellers, so this will be great exposure for you and your work.

Please include the phrase "purple cow" at the top of your bid.

If you have any questions, just let me know!

TWO DIFFERENT TYPES OF EDITING

It's important that you know what to look for when trusting someone you've never met to work on your book.

First off, editing goes much deeper than fixing a few comma splices here and there, or getting a second opinion on your manuscript.

You need to understand that editing comes in two different phases, covering two totally different sides of the spectrum.

Content Editing

The first of these two phases is content editing. As its name suggests, it has to do with fixing the content of your book. This will be more of a big picture edit, focusing on what you are saying and less on smaller, mechanical details.

During this phase, the focus is on the big picture. You and your editor will be asking questions like:

- Are there any holes in the book? (Which parts did I overlook?)
- How does the book flow? Are the transitions strong?
- How is the sequencing of the content? Which parts should be moved?
- What can I do to make this book better for the reader?
- What is unclear or needs even more clarification?
- What can be taken out to make the book better?

An editor will answer these questions from a different perspective: the reader's perspective.

Sometimes things make sense in your head that don't make sense to anyone else! (That doesn't mean you're crazy. It happens to the best of us). Your editor will be able to find the places that made sense to you but need more development for readers. Multiple perspectives will make the book so much better.

Copy Editing

After corrections are made to ensure the overall content is clear, it will be time to get down to the nitty-gritty—finding and mending little grammatical issues and punctuation errors.

During the copy editing stage, your editor will fix your spelling and grammar mistakes, help with redundancy and word choice, as well as give suggestions that make the overall text stronger on the sentence and word levels. In this stage, the editor combs through your book with a magnifying glass, so you don't have to.

Copy editing is essential to making your book stand above the rest. Even if the content is superior, having too many grammar, punctuation, or spelling errors will really distract your readers from the message you are trying to convey.

WHERE TO PRIORITIZE: CONTENT OR COPY EDITING?

When hiring your editor, you have the option to prioritize one phase of editing over the other.

The choice on whether to prioritize one over the other is ultimately yours. From your verbal read-throughs and your gut feeling about your manuscript, plus your budget, you can decide whether or not you need to emphasize one type of editing over the other.

Jeanine Phylisia, a first-time British novelist, soon came to the realization that her novel needed more of an extensive edit than she'd originally expected:

> My editor, Ana Young, not only cleaned up my entire novel, *Linemir's Tears*, but she taught me how to insert dialogue. Yes, I actually gave her my finished draft with relatively NO dialogue in it. It was my first sad attempt, and, thankfully, she was very gracious and kind. After Ana took a look at my draft, she informed me it was far from finished. I felt lost, but we soon came up with a system that worked for us, and we got to work immediately.

After finding a schedule that worked well for both of them, Jeanine and Ana worked steadily together for two weeks. In the end, the book was transformed into a simple, but special story. Jeanine and Ana now share what has turned into a lifelong friendship, all from one business partnership.

ABOUT COPYRIGHT

The good news for American writers is that copyright protection is automatically granted to your book, as long as your book is an original work. As stated on the US Copyright Office's site: "Your work is under copyright protection the moment it is created and fixed in a tangible form that it is perceptible either directly or with the aid of a machine or device." Essentially, once you've written your book, you don't have to actively apply for copyright protection. It's already there.

I recommend that writers outside of the US investigate your particular country's copyright protection laws. You may be required to apply for the protection.

TOO MANY COOKS . . .

When passing your book off to the editor, some people tend to think it's okay to pass their finished manuscripts off to anyone and everyone who wants to read it.

I've learned this the hard way: if you let too many people (or the wrong people) see your book, you are going to be running around trying to please a ton of people who likely do not have the most informed opinions.

For example, if I sent my how-to productivity guide for entrepreneurs to my grandma and she told me she didn't really like it, that would give me nothing to go off of. The book was not written for her, so yes she probably wouldn't like it. But that wouldn't mean it was bad. Someone in my target audience would probably think it was great and be able to give me more precise and helpful feedback.

So, if you choose to send your manuscript to any beta-readers (test readers who give you feedback), only send the book to people in your target audience. If the book pleases them, then you know it's on the right track.

In conclusion, carefully select the people who test read your book because too many cooks in the kitchen will do nothing but cause problems.

Once you are done with editing and the final draft of your book is one hundred percent solidified, you'll be ready to determine the title of your book as well as its cover image. Once you reach this point in the SPS 90-Day Way, give yourself some kudos!

The next stage in this process is pivotal. The title and cover images serve as a bridge, from the end point of the book creation phase over to the beginning point of the marketing phase (my personal favorite part of the SPS 90-Day Way!).

Do not get stressed because, as always, I'll be explaining it all and walking with you over this very important bridge.

Chapter 10

THE TITLE SAYS IT ALL

While the editor is busy working magic on your manuscript, you will be doing some work of your own. In your case, you will be creating the title of your book.

While many see titles as very intimidating, I recommend thinking of it this way—your title and subtitle are not hidden in some far-off universe that you can only locate after five years of focused labor with the aid of a specialty team of NASA engineers.

Why?

You know the content of your book better than anyone else, so you already know your title. It is there in your brain, and you've likely written it a few times already in the book itself.

WHERE TO START?

When you are coming up with a title, think of the main benefit of your book. Ask yourself, "What is the one thing I want people to walk away with when they read my book? What problem does this book solve?"

Crafting a title is all about surfacing the benefits your book has to offer. People are naturally self-interested and will primarily care about what your book can do for them and why they should read it. For this reason, your title must provide this information—*what* your book can do for readers and *why* they should be interested in it.

To understand this principle in another way, look at it through the lens of this common saying: "It's easier to sell pain pills than vitamins." This means people will jerk out their wallets in half a second to get rid of their pain, but they tend to be dismissive of preventing future pain. Your book title should center around the greatest "pain points" that your book solves for readers: *what* your book can do for readers and *why* they should be interested in it.

So, first figure out your target audience's biggest pain point, and in the title, call out a solution to that pain.

THE TALK-IT-OUT METHOD

Drawing out the benefits (the solutions to a reader's "pain") of your book is a lot easier than you might think. The best thing you can do is record a conversation with someone who literally knows nothing about your book.

Call a friend, family member, teacher, or neighbor, anyone that will listen to you talk about your book for ten to twenty minutes. You don't necessarily need to ask these people for advice on your title. You just need someone that will listen.

Again, make sure you record the conversation. Your aim is to explain the core of your book to your listener. Make sure you address the following:

o   whom the book is written for (a.k.a. your avatar or ideal reader)

o   what the book is about

o   the biggest takeaway(s) for the reader

o   why people will want to buy your book

As you talk, you will notice that you repeat yourself unintentionally, reiterating a key message that is essential for your listener to comprehend in order to fully understand your book. That's when the most important part of your book will expose itself, and your title will surface.

DON'T GET CATCHY

A huge mistake people make when crafting a title is thinking they need something catchy and clever. The books that sell the most are the books that have obvious, "boring" titles, such as *How to Win Friends and Influence People* or *Think and Grow Rich*. Just from these titles, you know exactly what these books are about. And that's exactly what you want for your book.

So, save yourself some time and energy and don't run off to "title land" trying to think of some crazy, catchy, artsy title that doesn't tell potential buyers anything about your book.

Instead, start with the obvious. Write down the glaring. Be straightforward, so much so that your title reaches out and bangs people in the head with a frying pan.

Potential readers should know EXACTLY what is in your book in a matter of seconds, simply by skimming your title.

THE DIFFERENCE—TITLE VS. SUBTITLE

When you are crafting a title for your book, your one job is to pique potential readers' interest and hit on a pain point. However, when you are crafting your subtitle, your job is to tell potential readers what your book is about and sell them on your message.

You are telling people what they *want* to hear. Not what they *need* to hear (remember—pain relief pills over vitamins).

Take one of my other books, Book Launch: *How to Write, Market & Publish Your First Bestseller in Three Months or Less AND Use It to Start AND Grow a Six-Figure Business*, for example. By reading this title and subtitle, readers know exactly what they are getting: best-seller status in three months or less and the foundation for a six-figure business.

This is specific and unambiguous, but I still make a bold claim, implying that by buying this book, readers are going to be able to start six-figure businesses. In turn, I've given them something to believe in, thus, selling them on a message.

Does everyone who's ever read *Book Launch* run a six-figure business within a couple of months? No. But reading *Book Launch* and writing their first books gives readers the tools to get there.

You want to do exactly the same thing with your subtitle. You want to be so niched down and precise that it makes you uncomfortable because you fear you are being too limiting. I want you to step out of your comfort zone completely. Once you break the barrier of your comfort zone, you will be in a place where the real magic happens.

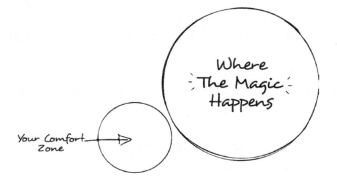

If your title and subtitle combo makes you want to poop your pants because it is just that bold, then they've found a winner. If it doesn't, then you need to go back to the drawing board.

It's only when you are this bold and uncomfortable that you will successfully compose a title that will sell.

BEFORE AND AFTER EXAMPLES

Below, in *Subtitle One*, we see the use of vague words that can basically be applied to any self-help book. You can read this subtitle and still know nothing about the book it applies to. This is exactly what you do *not* want.

Subtitle One (Before)	Subtitle Two (After)
Activate Your Dreams, Create Solutions, and Achieve Success	3 Simple Steps for Re-Sparking Your Buried Dreams and Building a Plan That Finally Works
A Way to Get Fit and Happy for Older People	The Senior Citizens' 5-Step Solution for a Stronger Brain and Body
How to Create Good Habits and Change Your Mindset and Your Life	How to Get Up from Rock Bottom, Create Habits to Love Yourself, and Learn toMaintain a Growth Mindset

However, after applying the advice given in this chapter, *Subtitle Two* tells potential readers exactly what each book is going to do for them and WHY they should read it. It tells them the specific pain points the book is going to address and alleviate.

Coming up with your title and subtitle can be really fun, if you let it. You just have to keep a few things in mind, know what potential readers really want to hear, and get so specific and bold that it makes you really uncomfortable.

In a few chapters, I will discuss using your title as a marketing tool, one that so many debut authors underutilize. The title is what gets buyers' attention. It is the instant "relate or don't relate" feeling people get when looking for a book.

Along with the title's striking ability to garner buyer's attention is the book cover. If you place your title on a shoddy book cover, all your hard work will be for nothing. These two aspects of authorship go hand in hand. If one isn't done correctly, they are both severely weakened. However, if your title and cover complement one another, your book will stand head and shoulders above your toughest competition.

So let's address the cover. I want to give you the tools to ensure yours is spot-on.

Chapter 11

JUDGING A BOOK BY ITS COVER

Right after you title your book, the next logical step is the development of a book cover. Your book cover is the physical proof of all your hard work. This is when your book becomes real. Through it, you finally see all of your ideas come to life.

It's a huge victory to arrive at this point, so please don't be tempted to rush it. It is worth the effort to put in the time to do it right.

We all know the saying, "Don't judge a book by its cover," and you and I both would like to believe it's true. However, take it from me, when people are in the market for a new book, that's EXACTLY what they are doing! Your book cover is the buyer's first impression of your work. You need this cover to represent your book's message and be designed in a way to capture your target audience's attention.

"Good enough" or "basically works" is not what you are aiming for here. Instead, set your sights on "knocks the socks off" and "in the bag." Your book cover should be your Sunday best, not your Monday morning worst. And to achieve the best, I'll show you a few key things you can do to get a cover that makes your book stand out from the crowd.

ANATOMY OF A WINNING BOOK COVER

There is a big difference between a "good-looking" cover and a "good-selling" cover. Some covers are "ugly" but sell well, while other covers "look good" but don't sell at all.

You might not necessarily think the cover of your book is a masterpiece, but you have to make your cover marketable—clean and crisp with the title big and bold. It should act as an advertisement for your book, not a piece of art.

A trick I like to use when deciding on a cover is to shrink the potential cover to the size of a postage stamp, which is the size of covers on online book retailer sites.Then line it up amongst other covers to see if it stands out.

When you try this with your cover choice, you'll find it helps you determine whether or not it pops.

And yes, we are looking for the highest level of *pop*!

BEST-SELLING AUTHOR TIP!
Contrary to popular belief, a powerful, best-selling cover does not necessarily include an image on it. Some people think there must be an image on the cover—a place, an object, the author, something— in order to attract potential readers to the book. This is not true.

CREATING A DESIGN BRIEF AND FINDING A DESIGNER FOR YOUR BOOK COVER

The Design Brief
As you've probably guessed, your book cover is not a DIY project. Just as you will work with an editor in the editing phase of your book, here you will be hiring a cover designer.

You will be writing a detailed project description for your cover designer called a "design brief," to establish the standards you are seeking for the design of your book cover.

In your design brief, you must tell the designer EXACTLY what you want. Be as detailed as possible. The more specific you are, the less that is left to guessing. For example, check out the detailed design brief I designed for *How to Not SUCK At Writing Your First Book*:

Book Title: **How To Not SUCK at Writing Your First Book**
Author's Name: Chandler Bolt

How To Not SUCK at Writing Your First Book is a book filled with proven solutions, options, and problem-solving methods that every first-time author needs to know—no matter what writing challenges they face.

The goal of the book is to stand out on the Amazon platform as a small thumbnail, as well as a 5.5 x 8.5 book with 72" spine.

The imagery should make the viewer feel that the book (and the author) are the authority in self-publishing and becoming a first-time author.

The reader should feel that they must have this book if they are thinking of writing a book but hate writing, aren't good at writing, or dream of writing a book but simply think they do not have the time. It's more important that the book "pops off the shelf" or stands out and catches the eye quickly.

The most important part of the design is that it sells, not that it looks pretty or well-designed. I am open to any image or illustration you choose. Here are a few words that come to mind when thinking of my book: growth, escape, satisfying, content, freedom, passion, motivation, success, author, writer, goals, accomplished.

I like a bold color palette. I like bold titles that you know right away what the title is and what it is about, not too busy and with simple color schemes. 2–3 colors.

Books with covers I like:
The Why of Work by David Ulrich
The Productive Person by Chandler Bolt & James Roper
The Power of Habit
Zero to One
Habit Stacking: 97 Small Life Changes That Take Five Minutes or Less

If you want to see the top three cover designs that resulted from this design brief, you'll find them in Chapter Fourteen (Keep reading and you'll see what I mean!).

Later in this chapter, you'll find a design brief template you can use to ensure you've got all the necessary bases covered when you reach this stage in the process.

Providing clear guidelines helps ensure the designer understands what you want. Plus, it merely eliminates time wasted in the creating of covers you don't like.

Shreya Kundu, a student at Self-Publishing School, wrote *Lizbang*, a collection of six interrelated short stories. The protagonists of the stories for various reasons experience powerful, life-altering transformations. Important themes in *Lizbang* include the transformational power of forgiveness, self-acceptance, and love. With this said, Shreya had to find the best cover possible for her book.

Below are the top three cover options she was choosing from. Notice that in each, the title stands out and the image supports the title rather than stealing from it. They all look very professional (not like something that was put together on Microsoft Paint). In the end, Shreya decided to go with the first one (yellow on gray).

Here are some other top-of-the-line covers from writers who followed the SPS 90-Day Way. Notice in each how prominent the titles are:

Tommy Baker, one of my mentors, once shared with me a valuable piece of business-related advice—you can never spend too much money on two things: a good accountant and a good lawyer. They will always pay for themselves.

In book writing, marketing, and publishing, the same is true for a good cover designer. So invest your time and money in finding a first-rate designer, one who can take a short description of your book and make a cover of gold.

The Designer
Once you have your design brief, the next step is to submit your request to one of these designing platforms:

Option 1—Fiverr
Although you have a couple choices here (and they will become outdated eventually) for finding designers, a good place to start is a website called Fiverr. This is a solid option, and it's relatively cheap. On Fiverr, for less than twenty dollars, you can find a competent designer who will create a winning cover.

Fiverr, in a nutshell, is a site where you can get a ton of stuff done for just five bucks.

If you decide to go with Fiverr for your book cover, go to http://fiverr.com, type "book covers" in the search bar, and browse the "Gigs" that are offered. Once you find some designers you like, click on the "High Rating" tab and search for designers who have great ratings and have done tons of gigs.

Read the reviews and see what people are saying about particular designers. Once you find these top-rated designers, buy several gigs (around three or so) for about twenty dollars total.

Option 2—99designs

Another place to get some great book covers is 99designs.

99designs uses a tiered pricing structure where a minimum of fifteen to thirty designers will submit designs for the chance to "win the job."

Basically, you put together a design brief, create a portfolio, and submit it. Then designers will start sending designs to you right away.

99designs also provides a platform to rate the designs. You can create a poll to share your favorites on social media, such as Facebook, and have people vote on which of your favorite design choices they prefer.

This not only gives you feedback but also generates interest in your book, which is very important and something I'll be going into in-depth in the chapters on marketing.

If you decide to go with 99designs, here are the necessary steps to take:

o   Pick two designs you really like.

o   Pick one more design you think is marketable
    (even if you don't love it).

o   Share all three covers everywhere you possibly can
    (Facebook, Twitter, Instagram).

o   Ask for feedback on the covers.

Ultimately, it's a judgment call on your part, but getting feedback in the early stages of your book creation process greatly helps the launching of your book.

BEST-SELLING AUTHOR TIP!

When it is time to publish your book, online book retailers like Amazon will only accept certain image formats: GIF (or .gif), PNG (or .png), BMP (or .bmp), and JPEG (or .jpeg). Check in with your design artist to make sure your cover design is saved in the appropriate format.

Option 3—Find a Freelance Designer

Below is a design brief template you can use if you decide to go with a freelance designer instead of one of the sites I already mentioned. Feel free to use this brief and change it around to best fit your needs.

You can send off your request to have your cover designed on 99designs or Fiverr, but you can also branch out and use this same template on Upwork, your personal network, and other similar websites.

Book Title:
Author's Name:

....is a book about ....

The goal of the book is to stand out on the online book retailer platform as a small thumbnail, as well as a 5.5 x 8.5 book with 72" spine.

The imagery should make the viewer feel that the book (and the author) is the authority on the topic of...

....

The reader should feel that they must have this book if they are.............
.... It's more important that the book "pops off
the shelf" or stands out and catches the eye quickly.

The most important part of the design is that it sells, not that it looks pretty
or well-designed. I am open to any image or illustration you choose. Here
are a few words that come to mind when thinking of my book:.......................
....

I like a bold color palette. I like bold titles that you know right away
what the title is and what it is about, not too busy and with simple
color schemes. 2–3 colors.

Books with covers I like:
The Why of Work by David Ulrich
The Productive Person by Chandler Bolt and James Roper
The Power of Habit
Zero to One
Habit Stacking: 97 Small Life Changes That Take Five Minutes or Less
Launch: An Internet Millionaire's Secret Formula To Sell Almost Anything
Online, Build A Business You Love, And Live The Life Of Your Dreams

BEST-SELLING AUTHOR TIP!
This might be a blow to your ego, but . . . your name, unless you are a
well-known author, should be a smaller size on your book cover. You
want buyers' attention focused on the title and subtitle (how they can
benefit from reading your book) instead of your name.

DONE IS BETTER THAN PERFECT
(YES, THAT APPLIES HERE TOO)

Let's take a moment to revisit one of our go-to mantras—DONE IS
BETTER THAN PERFECT.

If for some reason you've settled on a cover that you discover, later on, isn't quite right, you simply change it at that later stage, even after you've published your book. Yes, you can do this. It's one of the many perks of self-publishing.

As I touched on earlier, determining your title and cover image close the door on the book creation process and, at the same time, open the door to book marketing. Titles and covers require you to wear both a writer's hat and a marketer's hat. So, at this stage, whether you are aware of it or not, you've already placed the marketer's hat on your head.

By this point, you will already be two-thirds finished with your trek with only the marketing remaining. It's now time to transition completely and deliberately into the marketing of your book.

INSPIRATIONAL INTERLUDE

Never in a million years would Shirley Wu have dreamed of becoming a published author, of not just one, but two books, with more to come.

For years she'd had varying degrees of success breaking into the holistic health world. Shirley knew she had a lot of knowledge stemming from personal experience, but her knowledge was typically limited to an audience of just family and friends occasionally asking her for advice.

After personally overcoming post traumatic stress disorder (PTSD), helping people in their healing journey felt like her calling in life, but she didn't know how to move from hobbyist to a voice of authority. "I felt like I could deliver value to even more people who could benefit from the information, but didn't know how to achieve that," Shirley shared.

To establish herself as an expert and attract clients to her business, Shirley decided to write a book. She carefully followed the SPS 90-Day Way to publish *The Girl Who Roars*. Although Shirley had no social media following whatsoever, she was still able to hit #1 on the Amazon charts on the first day of her launch.

"Just because you don't use social media doesn't mean you can't be a self-published author," declares Shirley with pride. "I texted a picture of my book cover to all of my friends and family, prompting them to download on launch day and share my book on their social media." Shirley also visited local businesses that she thought would be interested in her topic and got them to share as well.

She finds comfort in the fact that her books, *The Girl Who Roars* and *Resurgence of a Fallen Angel*, are still out there, spreading her message without the need of social media or an extensive technological background promoting them.

If you find yourself in this situation, marketing and launching a book without a social media network to back you, just remember Shirley. Shirley was able to do it, so can you!

Section 3

PRE-LAUNCH

Chapter 12

THE MARKETING MACHINE

Decades ago, farmers growing "Chinese gooseberries" had a problem: nobody wanted to buy their odd-looking yet delicious fruit. It was the height of the Cold War, and the name proved a marketing nightmare.

First, the name reminded people of Red China, i.e., the Communist enemy. On top of that, gooseberry sounded weird and gross. The two-word name sounded both menacing and disgusting, so naturally no one wanted to eat it.

And then suddenly, everything changed for the Chinese gooseberry. One genius marketer realized the Chinese gooseberry fruit bore a strange resemblance to the fuzzy brown kiwi, New Zealand's national bird.

The rest is history: the Chinese gooseberry was named the "kiwifruit," sales skyrocketed, and now almost all of us have tried the small, delicious fruit.

What's the lesson here? How you position a product makes all the difference in the world. And this isn't just true for fruits. It works for books too. The very first part of marketing your book is positioning it so people will have no problem paying for what you are asking for it.

As we transition into talking about book marketing, I'll start with a confession—I'm a marketer at heart. I've spent tens of thousands of my own dollars on conferences, seminars, books, and courses to learn exactly how to be a great marketer, and especially how to market books successfully.

I have launched five books and helped hundreds of regular people launch their own books successfully. From the mistakes I've made, successes I've had, and the tons of research I've done, I have learned exactly what works (and what doesn't).

Everything I'm about to teach you on book marketing is something I've tested myself. I'm teaching from experience, NOT from theory. Over the years, I've developed, tweaked, and perfected a book marketing system that works for anyone . . . even if you're someone who considers yourself to be horrible at marketing (and it makes you cringe).

In the chapters to come, I'll be teaching you everything you need to know and nothing you don't. I'm sharing with you the same marketing practices I personally used to successfully launch my five books and to grow my business from $0 to $1.3M in a year, using books as the foundation.

When it comes to marketing, people usually fall in one of two camps:

1. People who love it, work at it, and make it look easy
2. People who hate it, avoid it, and feel like they're selling their souls

Sadly, most people fall in the latter category. They see marketing as this slimy activity that's hard, mysterious, and only occupied by people with bad intentions.

The reality is, this couldn't be farther from the truth. It's just a story that we've told ourselves (or that others have forced upon us).

If you believe in what you're selling, marketing isn't a grungy activity. It's a way to get your message in the hands of more people.

It should go without saying that if you're writing a book on something, you believe in it. If not, you probably wouldn't write the book in the first place. Now that you've written about something you believe in, it's time to get it in the hands of as many people as possible.

It doesn't matter which camp you find yourself in because in the chapters to come, I'll break down book marketing in a way that's easy to understand and easy to implement.

Simply focus on following the step-by-step approach I'm about to give you. You don't have to follow it perfectly, and it may not be easy at first. But if you stick with it, I promise you'll find success.

A BIG PICTURE VIEW OF THE MARKETING PHASE

When you reach this point in the process, you will be anywhere from three weeks to a couple of months away from launching your book. You will have spent the previous sixty days or so working for this moment—preparing to launch your book.

In this final section, I am going to walk you through the positioning, marketing, and launching of your book, so you reach the best-selling status you're aiming for. I'll be presenting a multi-layered marketing approach in which you'll build anticipation for your book weeks before you launch it (instead of waiting until right before launch like most people do).

My special approach consists of various moving parts that, once set into action, create an awesome marketing machine. These moving parts, that I'll be carefully presenting, include:

o *Assembling a Launch Team*
    Yes, you can wipe the sweat off your brow. It is more than just you doing the marketing of your book. I'm going to show you how to assemble, utilize, and lead a group of people of your choosing to help you in this final phase.

o *The Building Buzz Strategy*
    I am going to show how you and your team can build anticipation for your book weeks before you launch it. Even if you are not familiar with social media or tech savvy at all, with my suggestions and the help of your launch team, you'll succeed in building some serious hype around your book.

o *How to Turn Book Buyers Into Email Subscribers*
Some of you are seeking book buyers who will do more than just read your book. You want these people to start with your book and then move on to donate money to a related cause or go to your website and buy another product or service from you. I will show you exactly what to do to go from book purchase to a higher priced purchase with you or your business.

o *Four Ways to Launch*
I'll also present four different launch strategies for successfully launching your book. For each option, I'll cover who should use it, its pros and cons, as well as the complete steps for putting it to action. I will provide you with everything you need, so you'll find success no matter which strategy you choose.

o *Leveraging Launch Week*
I will supply you with specifically timed techniques to employ during your launch week to ensure it is a success. An excellent trajectory ensues from a powerful start.

o *Tapping Into an Existing Ecosystem: Amazon Juice, Reviews, and Downloads*
Amazon chooses to promote certain products within its site and beyond. I call this Amazon promotion, the "Amazon juice." While Amazon keeps private the exact characteristics it draws on for deciding which products to promote, I know there are a few key things you can do to successfully tap into their ecosystem of 100 million+ buyers and to make your book stand out. I'll be teaching you my best strategies for maximizing book sales, attention, and impact from your book.

THE RIFLE OVER THE SHOTGUN APPROACH

If you know anything about a shotgun, you know that each bullet contains dozens, if not hundreds of bb's or pellets. When a shotgun is fired, the pellets spread out, forming a wave of bullets, in the hopes that one or more of the pellets will strike the target.

A rifle, on the other hand, fires a singular bullet that can travel for long distances while maintaining superior accuracy and effectiveness.

When it comes to book marketing, most people follow the "shotgun approach." They make landing pages, Facebook pages, special Twitter accounts, paid advertising in certain online newspapers, and every other book marketing tactic they've heard of.

These people try to do everything under the sun to market their books, hoping that something works. This is what I call the "hope and pray" method (a.k.a. the shotgun approach).

What happens is they end up spreading their efforts too thin and spinning their wheels in an exhausting effort. The shotgun approach wastes time and doesn't yield significant results.

On the opposite end of the spectrum lies the "rifle approach." This approach is the core of what I'll be teaching you in the chapters to come. The rifle approach involves focus, aim, and direction.

The rifle approach in book marketing entails being very specific about where and to whom you put your marketing energy. For every marketing technique I give, you must remember to direct it at your target audience or at places (blogs, podcasts, websites, etc.) frequented by your target audience.

Be specific. Always keep in mind that niches equals riches when it comes to marketing and launching your book.

As we move into the book marketing section, I encourage you to put away the shotgun and get out the rifle. You have a specific message. You have a target audience, the avatar, that you wrote your book to. They are the bullseye that you will direct your efforts toward.

Chapter 13

NO "I" IN "TEAM"

Use a Launch Team to Spread Your Message and Sell More Books

In this marketing phase, it's not just techniques and information that you'll need to succeed, but also a little oomph. That's where Samantha Roose's story comes in.

Samantha Roose told me that she'd wasted a lot of time in her late teens and early twenties. She said she was "sitting in a puddle of tears waiting for someone to give [her] a map and a compass—when all [she] needed to do was identify the talents [she] already possessed and walk through the already-open doors."

Samantha's epiphany—to live fully in the present—propelled her to create a conference to teach and inspire young women to live with passion, vision, and purpose. After the great success of the conference, Samantha decided to craft her philosophy into a book. So, she buckled down and committed to the SPS 90-Day Way.

Samantha confessed, though, that when she reached the marketing phase, she was feeling stressed:

> The most intimidating part of my publishing *Such A Time* was by far the launch. I didn't know how to get people on my launch team. I didn't know how to get people to buy my book. That's where these simple steps saved the day. I didn't have any excuses. I had an outline. All I had to do was accomplish each daily task and trust the system.

Just as Samantha admitted, when it comes to marketing and launching your book, it is very common to feel intimidated. It's normal. Many first time authors feel this way. It's a big transition stepping out of the mindset of creative and into the mindset of selling.

That's why creating a launch team is so crucial. This small group of people that you've hand-picked will help you navigate these unknown waters. They'll share the burden with you. Together, you will pull off a stellar launch.

BIRD'S EYE VIEW OF A LAUNCH TEAM

In a nutshell, your launch team is a group of people, hand picked by you, who are eager to help market and make your book launch a triumph. Because they believe in you and your book, this team is going to give their time, ideas, skills, and networks to ensure that your book launch is a success.

Launch teams should reduce your stress, multiply your reach, expand the skills at your disposal, and, most importantly, take some responsibility off your shoulders.

Who are these people? How exactly are they going to be supporting you? Why would they give their time and energy like this? Let's start with these important questions.

THE "WHO" OF YOUR LAUNCH TEAM

Your book is delivering a particular message or story. For your launch team, you need to think about people who either care about that message/story or people who care about you. It is possible that many of these people will fit both criteria.

To figure out who should be on your launch team, start by thinking of the people in your closest circle, and the people connected to them, who care a lot about you, care a lot about the big message of your book, and/or want marketing experience—your spouse, siblings, children, cousins, in-laws, best friends, best friends' children or siblings, colleagues, colleagues' spouses, colleagues' family or friends, neighbors, and neighbors' friends and family.

Additionally, you need to consider people in outer circles. For instance, consider people from various stages in your life—high school, college, graduate school, your first job, your second job, your third job. The people whom you are friendly with but may not know you well from the routines you keep—8 a.m. coffee house buddies, the other dog owners at the dog park, the people in your Saturday morning CrossFit class, the other parents whom you converse with while waiting to pick up your child after daycare, the friendly people from your building whom you chat with in the mailroom, etc. Though you haven't seen some of these people in a while or don't see them often, they may very well be inspired by your book and want to help promote it.

THE "HOW" OF YOUR LAUNCH TEAM

The people you choose to be on your team are meant for more than taking care of small "busy work" tasks. They will allow you to capitalize on one to many marketing tactics:

o   Using their social media to draw attention to your book

o   Leaving positive book reviews on Amazon

o   Downloading your book from Amazon, even if they've received a PDF of it

o   Considering who in their circles would benefit from your book and informing those people of it

o   Contacting speciality blogs, magazines, newspapers, sites about new books, podcasts, YouTube channels or personalities, and Twitter personalities that either would be interested in your book or that gain attention from your ideal audience

o   Contacting relevant people and places at the local level that would be interested in promoting your book—local politicians, business leaders, educators, and community service leaders, as well as local clubs, churches, mosques, synagogues, nonprofit organizations, businesses, schools, and intramural sports teams or clubs.

o   Developing a high-quality Facebook page for your book

- o   Making related t-shirts, mugs, or magnets
- o   Making a series of short videos about your book and posting them online
- o   Establishing a Goodreads page about you and your book

THE "WHY" OF YOUR TEAM

Why people will join your launch team directly relates to the "who" I addressed previously. There will be those who simply love you and for that reason want to support you. There will be those who really believe in the message of your book and for that reason will want to support it. There will be the people who always wanted to write a book but haven't, and will want to support you because you've done it. There will be people who simply get a rush from marketing and/or working their social media followings and will find your book an innovative, new angle for doing so. Also, there will be people who will want to be privy to a behind-the-scenes-look at a book launch.

I firmly believe that people simply like to help other people. They like to be a part of something that they think matters beyond themselves. I know I do.

The point is that your launch team isn't helping you for nothing. Belonging, accomplishment, and significance matter to each of us, and being a part of your launch team will supply people with that.

MY FIRST LAUNCH TEAM

It wasn't until my brother Seth and I launched *Breaking Out of a Broken System* that I was truly able to see the power of a launch team.

Because the purpose of *Breaking Out of a Broken System* was to bring attention to a cause (the havoc malaria wreaks on people in the developing world), and to raise money for that cause, Seth and I were able to rally a lot of concerned people. We assembled an energetic and passionate launch team of a hundred people from all over the world. (Don't worry if you can't find one hundred people to be on your team. I'll address team size shortly.)

I was a little nervous about it because it seemed a big responsibility leading such a large team. However, the achievements that the launch team pulled off were greater than anything Seth and I could have managed alone. Let me share with you the accomplishments of a few superlative team members.

Jen Savits Badger, a launch team member for *Breaking Out of a Broken System*, designed t-shirts for every team member to wear and give away to others (at the end of the chapter I've included a picture of one). She saw the t-shirts as conversation starters, another way to spread the word about the book and cause. And the t-shirts were even more than that. They created greater team unity and increased our spirit and zest. Plus, they showed Jen's tremendous generosity.

Kelsey Kufner, a singer, songwriter, and music journalist from Wisconsin, held a benefit concert to bring attention to the cause and the book. Ten thousand people attended the concert. Kelsey raised money, sold books, and brought awareness about the devastation of malaria in the developing world to the 10 thousand concert attendees.

Chelsea Miller, a launch team member from West Virginia, put the icing on the cake in her contributions. She pulled off accomplishments you'd think only a seasoned PR pro could manage. Chelsea landed spots on two prominent national radio stations, K-LOVE and WALK-FM, for Seth and me to discuss the book and the cause. She scored us a front-page spread in *The Herald Dispatch*, West Virginia's main newspaper. She persuaded Nacho Followill, the manager of the internationally acclaimed rock band Kings of Leon, to promote *Breaking Out of a Broken System* amongst his large social media following.

When the message of your book resonates with people, they find it a privilege and a pleasure to spread the word. And, as I'll tell you repeatedly—one single, quality team member is more valuable to you and your launch than a truckload of undependable people.

LAUNCH TEAM CREATION AND FORMATION IN SEVEN STEPS

I am explaining the creation and formation of a launch team in seven vital steps presented in the order in which they need to be followed. Take your time and read through the steps carefully because this information is the scaffolding used to support the marketing of your book and, of course, your launch week.

Step 1: Determine the size of your launch team.

While there is no exact science to determining the perfect launch team size for everyone, there is one outstanding factor that can be used to help determine a good size for your team—the size of your following.

When I say "your following," what I mean is the people who are interested in you, your book, and/or your products. For some of you, this may mean the five or so friends and family you most regularly talk with on the phone, send emails to, or keep up with on social media. For others, especially those with established businesses or highly involved in organizations, your following is even larger.

You may have twenty, fifty, or several hundred people who keep up-to-date with what you are doing. Whether your following is a group of friends that you call each week on the phone or a large email list, somewhere out there, there is a group of people interested in what you are doing. This is your following.

It is from this following that you are going to recruit and select people to be on your team. For those of you with a small following aim for a ten- to fifty-person launch team. If you already have a solid following and a large email list and network, you should aim for anywhere between 100 to 250 team members. If you feel comfortable with the notion of "your following" and can readily identify these people, move on to the second step. If this concept is totally new to you and you are not convinced you have any following, please read on.

So You Think You Have No Following . . .

Let me start by saying that all those people with a substantial following at one point in their lives were where you are at now—just starting out and with no following. So they had to do what you are going to be doing—build one.

By this point, you should realize that you know a lot of people, and it is likely that some of those people will be interested enough in you, your book, or even marketing itself to want to work with you. The next thing you need to do is briefly speak to them to gauge their interest level. And if you can detect any interest, you then proceed with giving them your contact details and proposing that they be on your launch team.

Here's an example for putting out feelers, gauging interest, and locating people to be on your launch team:

Oh, I'm fine. What about you—how are you doing?

I'm actually feeling pretty good. I've spent the last two months writing my first book. My editor and I finished the final draft two weeks ago. Just getting together my launch strategy now.

Congratulations. A book. I've always wanted to write a book myself. What did you write—the great American novel?

No, nothing like that. It's actually a book for longtime runners who are suffering from knee trouble but don't want to have to stop running. I've got a lot of experience in the area. In my book I tell people my story, how I came out on the other side. What I did and do.

Yeah, I heard that can be an issue. I don't run, but my wife does. She actually runs with a friend who's had knee problems.

I'd love to have your wife and her friend check out my book. Maybe they'd even want to help me launch it. Here's my email address. I'd love it if they shot me an email, so I can share an excerpt with them.

Sure. I'll pass it along.

With lots of determination on your part, you will simply drop these kinds of feelers at every opportunity, and slowly but surely you'll find the two, three, or four people who believe in your message and want to be on your team.

And, as I'm about to explain in the second step, it's not the size of your team that matters most. It's the kind of people who are on it.

Step 2: Recruit and select reliable team members.
The biggest lesson I have learned is QUALITY > QUANTITY when it comes to a launch team. You want to make sure you have a team that will actually help you launch your book and not just sign up to seem supportive, get free stuff (if that's a possibility), or feel included but not want to actually do anything.

Recruitment
If you are someone that thinks you have no following, I already laid out your recruitment strategy in the first step. So please skip to "Clear Expectations."

Those of you with followings, small or large, can simply send out a mass email or message to recruit followers to join your launch team. You'll describe your book, establish clear expectations (see below) about the role, and present the selection process (see below) in the message.

Clear Expectations
When you are recruiting people for your team, you want them to be psyched to participate and super enthusiastic about the project and launch, but you also need to be upfront about what the role involves. At the minimum, you should set the expectation that each team member read your book, write a review for it on day one of its release, spread the word about it to their friends and communities, and contribute a designated amount of time each week for x number of weeks (you fill in the "x") to work on the launch.

Selection
Again, one quality team member is worth more than any number of unreliable members. And, believe it or not, there is actually a one-size-fits-all solution to making sure you select only the top players for your launch team:

MAKE THEM APPLY!

Even if you are in the I-don't-think-I-have-a-following camp, this still applies to you. You may choose to go about the applying in a less formal manner than I'm suggesting, but you should still do it. Why? You want quality.

The Application
Requiring your candidates to fill out an application has many perks, one of which is making your eventual team members feel like they are part of an exclusive club and their "acceptance" will make them feel more valued. It also lets you do a bit of screening before you let someone in on any book secrets.

Most importantly, it sets a precedent with close friends or family members who want to help but may not realize the seriousness and importance of the launch. Remember, you want to make sure the people on your team are in alignment with your vision and values.

To effectively use an application system, send out the application at least ONE MONTH before your launch date, and give applicants exactly ONE WEEK to apply. This will give you a few days to screen through the applications and make decisions.

Here's a list of recommended questions for your application:

o Why are you interested in supporting the launching of [Book Title]? What about [Book Title] most speaks to you?

o What are some specialized skills or characteristics you have that you want to contribute to this book launch?

o What is your time commitment to this?
Name some influential people you can reach out to that you think will be very interested in [Book Title]. Also, please be sure to give a little background info about them and why you think they'd be interested in [Book Title].

Additionally, to generate interest as you form your team, you can even offer some benefits for joining, such as a free copy of the book, the inclusion of team members' names in the "Acknowledgments" part of your book, a behind-the-scenes look at your writing process, or hosting a one-hour exclusive webinar just for team members.

The best part is, you don't have to offer anything that costs you monetarily when trying to incentivise people to join your team. The most compelling reason why people will want to join is what I wrote previously: if they believe in your book, then it will be their pleasure to be on your team. People like to be a part of something that they think matters beyond themselves.

Step 3: Establish communication standards early on.
Finding an effective line of communication between you and your team members is the secret to any successful launch team.

You will need to communicate frequently to keep your team engaged. I recommend that two or three weeks prior to the launch, you send at least one email per week and many during the actual launch week. For instance, you will send emails regarding weekly tasks, progress reports, shout-outs, success stories, innovative ideas, general information, etc.

You are essentially the coach of the team, so it's not just a matter of allocating tasks and ensuring they are informed or on-task; you must also keep everyone's energy and motivation up, reminding them that they are a part of something special, something that matters.

How can you do this? Send inspiring quotations, goofy photos, or short videos. Create contests or activities to build rapport...maybe even a rap contest, with your book as the subject of the lyrics.

The second and most vital piece of the communication puzzle is creating a private Facebook group as a home for your team members. The private Facebook group will be used for engaging the team, sharing ideas, and posting feedback, progress reports, shout-outs, and success stories. This is where the "one-to-many" announcements will be made. Also, it makes it easy for individuals to connect with each other inside the team and share ideas.

Remember to keep everything you do *personal* when communicating with team members. PEOPLE ARE PEOPLE, and you need to treat them like it—don't ask them to promote everything and don't allocate tasks to them as if they are your underlings. Use your requests strategically and always make your team feel appreciated, every step of the way!

Step 4: Create a welcome video/post.
While you are waiting for the applications to roll in, you will have a couple days of downtime. During these couple of days, it is time to create a welcome video/post for the people accepted to be on your launch team.

Use the welcome video as a "pinned post" at the top of the Facebook page. This is where you need to set the community culture and start to build rapport with the members.

Suggested topics to cover in the welcome video/post:

1. Congratulate applicants for getting selected and express gratitude for their willingness.

2. Clearly state expectations for team member behavior.

3. State your mission/purpose for writing your book, and explain why you want to share it with as many people as you can.

4. Set expectations for what is to come leading up to the book launch.

In the video, feel free to read members' responses to the application questions, "Why are you interested in supporting the launching of [Book Title]? What about [Book Title] most speaks to you?" In doing so, you can really inspire, motivate, and create team unity.

Encourage your team members to be active—commenting, engaging, and posting feedback in the group. Make sure to remind members to freely reach out to you with any creative marketing ideas.

Step 5: Determine the launch team's assignments and weekly tasks.
One of the most effective ways to use your team is to give them weekly assignments in the private Facebook group.

During the week you accept applications, you will also want to start planning what types of weekly tasks you'll need team members to help you with.

Some successful tasks I've used (in this order) in the past include:

o Reading a copy of the book and providing feedback

o Reaching out to relevant bloggers and influencers

o Promoting the book on their social media and other relevant social media forums

o Downloading the book on launch day (to get that Amazon juice going. I'll return to this later in the book)

o Writing reviews on launch day

Step 6: Utilize team members' talents.

While you don't want to bombard your team with tasks, there are going to be some people who want to do more than necessary for you and your book, and are willing to spend more time helping.

These people will be key players in your launch, and you will want to draw attention to how awesome they are doing.
You can ask for volunteers by simply writing a post during the introductory week for your team and asking:

> Would anyone like to go above and beyond (more than you already have)? If you have any special talents, please comment on this post and let me know. Here is the type of thing I'm looking for . . .

Examples of What You Can Ask for Help With

- o Spicing up your one-page book description
- o Checking for formatting errors and the readability of your book
- o Making graphics to spread on social media
- o Making promotional videos
- o Spreading the message with a member's large network

Step 7: Have fun and don't forget to thank your team!

Having a launch team will not only lead to a great launch but will also build great relationships that will last well beyond launch day. All you need to do is make the effort to stay engaged with your team. After all, these people are giving you their support for nearly a month.

When your launch is all said and done, don't forget to thank your team for everything they did to help you! Don't hold back on showing them gratitude—individual thank-you emails, handwritten thank-you letters, group thank-you posts, and lots of shout-outs to individuals.

Reward your team and yourself for all the success you had together.

Launch teams, when done correctly, give you the foundation to make your book a success even before it launches. Instead of carrying all the responsibility alone, you now have a team of people behind you, supporting your book and its success.

If you utilize the talent within the team, set up a good communication system, know what to ask of your team, and carefully choose the members, you will find that creating a launch team is one of the most powerful ways to successfully market your book.

The next three chapters of this book are dedicated to making sure your launch goes off without a hitch. As you read the chapters and implement the strategies, think to yourself, "How can my launch team support me in implementing this advice?"

-¡- BONUS -¡-

One of the most overlooked benefits of having a launch team is the relationships you will build. When people are grouped together for a single cause they believe in, it's like they become a family overnight.

Because of these great relationships, launch teams frequently never stop giving.

I have personally ended up hiring people from my launch teams, and they have continued to buy additional products from me long after the launch of the book.

As a launch team group begins to establish itself, encourage some of the random fun things that your launch team might do.

Here are some examples of little things my launch team did without me having to ask, things which kept the launch interesting, bonded us even more, and kept the energy high.

Nacho Followill and Chelsea Miller Supporting #1book1life

Hi guys! So, as some of you might know, I hosted a benefit concert this past Sunday for Breaking Out of a Broken System and PMI. It was a huge success! We were small but mighty- we raised $682 for PMI and sold 12 books! With the donations still rolling in, right now we're at about $702! I am so proud and so moved to be a part of it all. Seth and Chandler, thank you from the bottom of my heart for letting me be a part of this crew, I am in awe of the mountains we're moving! All of you have changed my life!

P.S. Here's a quick video from Sunday, check it out!

Here is the link for the shirts. Orders will be taken only through this method to keep things simple and organized. We'll announce the design choice for the back of the shirts tomorrow morning, but wanted to allow you all to begin placing your orders so we can get going on ordering apparel. We'll go into production in the next few days. Thanks so much!

Breaking Out of a Broken System launch team shirts

Product specifications: JERZEES HEAVYWEIGHT BLEND TEE Black with bright yellow and white ink, full front and back graphic Men's sizing 5.6-ounce, 50/50 cotton/poly (preshrunk) 1x1 rib knit crew collar Seamless body with set-in...

SQUAREUP.COM

Sometimes the swim is easy, sometimes you're treading water, and sometimes you just feel like you're sinking. But if an elephant can sink into the water and rise back to the top, so can you! The dreams placed in your heart weren't put there to tease you. Land may look like it's far away, but keep swimming.

—Seth Bolt "Breaking Out of a Broken System"

For a more in-depth look at how both my students and I run launch teams, go here: http://self-publishingschool.com/s/ap-1

Chapter 14

BUILDING BUZZ BEFORE YOUR BOOK LAUNCH

The Hero's Journey as a Marketing Strategy

THE HERO'S STORY

Think of any Will Smith movie you have ever seen. I use Will Smith as an example because his characters usually follow the iconic "hero's journey" story structure (think *The Pursuit of Happiness*).

In the first act, normal life gets interrupted by a terrible event, the hero is called to action, and then the hero connects with a mentor or secondary character.

In the second act, the hero goes through trials and tribulations, has a crisis of meaning (the part where he almost gives up), and eventually defeats the antagonist.

It isn't until the third act that the hero has a transformation (or revelation) due to the events he went through in act two. After he comes to terms with his revelation, he then is truly able to return to his normal life as a changed man accompanied by his new outlook on life.

THE AUTHOR-HERO'S JOURNEY

When you are writing your book, you become the hero of your own story. It may not always feel like it to you, especially when the going gets tough, but in the eyes of everyone around you, they're excitedly cheering you on through this challenging, but life-transforming process ... just like they would root for any hero while watching a movie.

The key to building buzz is creating a story to go along with your writing journey for everyone to follow. In this story, you share and celebrate with your followers each step of your "author-hero's writing journey." And it is through this story, you get people in your network involved and make them feel like a part of your team. Thus, this is where and how your buzz building occurs.

The author-hero's writing journey will be presented in three acts. As you go through these acts, I will show you some places where you can share your quest with your network to stealthily build buzz for your book.

Act I

You've been living an ordinary life for a while when suddenly you've been called upon to go on a quest. In your commitment to write a book via the SPS 90-Day Way, you show you've accepted the quest. Plus, you've met with your mentor (this book).

Building Buzz: So, how do you leverage your move from the ordinary to extraordinary to stealthily build buzz? Start by sending out or posting a picture of yourself holding *Published.* along with a proclamation that you have decided to write a book.

Act II

As you've already read, you will face many trials and tribulations on your book writing journey. Times will get hard, but you know how to overcome them. For example, you will endure a crisis of meaning in the revision and editing stage. But you will overcome it by getting your completed draft back from the editor.

Building Buzz: At each of these milestone events, you want to inform and include your network in any way that you can. Post on social media, send out emails, or text/call your friends.

Act III

Act three begins with a transformation. This is when you transition into the marketing mindset and begin to think and act like a marketer.

Shortly after this "scene" is when you begin the launch process of your book and return back to the people in your network that have been following your book from the second you started the journey in act one. (More on how to do this later in the chapter.)

Finally, after the launch of your book has died down, you return to life with the wisdom only an author holds. You have achieved your goals, and your life will never be the same. More opportunities, options, and relationships have opened to you. Perhaps, you'll even go on another quest.

A lot of people think marketing doesn't start until after your book is completed. The truth is, it actually starts the moment you decide to write your book.

THE WHAT AND WHEN

I know I've already stated this, but it deserves repeating: because this is a strategy that builds, you need to be trickling out information about your book long before you release it. For example, on the day you commit to the SPS 90-Day Way, (thus ninety days before book launch), begin building buzz. How? Read on!

As I wrote above, the "what" you are trickling out is the story of your author-hero's journey. You will share the significant milestones, trials, tribulations, and triumphs you encounter on your journey.

In building buzz, when you share the triumphs and tribulations of your book writing journey, use email or social media. Call people on the phone. Send out text messages. Do what you have to do to reach your people.

Consider sharing the following events:

Decide to Write a Book	Tell everyone you know that you've made the decision to write a book.
Start Writing	Tell everyone the day you start writing and when you plan to have things completed.
Finish Your First Chapter	This is a huge win and your friends should help you celebrate!
Finish Your Rough Draft	This is an even bigger win; make a huge deal about this and tell everyone you know.
Finish Editing the Book	This part of the process can be tough. Tell your following when you have a finalized manuscript.
Cover Competition	Involve your following by having them vote on their favorite cover.
Share the Results	Tell your following which cover won.
Pre-Release	Tell your following when the book is free and how to get it.
Launch Day	Tell your following launch day has arrived and you need their help.
Launch Week Celebration	Share the success of your book and exciting stats from the launch.
Launch Week "Thank You"	Thank everyone who helped you during launch week.
Successful PR	If you reach any of your personal marketing goals, like landing a mention in a newspaper or getting an invite to do an interview, share it with your network.

Over time, all the tidbits you've been sharing will lead to your followers feeling more than just included on your journey. They will become emotionally invested in helping you achieve the big end goal, i.e., successfully launching your book.

Once they feel invested in the project, when it comes time for you to ask something of them, like leaving book reviews or downloading your book, they will be eager to take the time to do it.

An Example
When I released the paperback version of *The Productive Person*, rather than simply telling people we were about to release the paperback version in the next couple of months, James posted this on Facebook when we got our demo copy:

This was a fun, goofy way of letting people know the book was coming out, without actually telling them directly.

Another Example
When I've held cover design competitions, I often start them already knowing which is the best cover (in my opinion)—and I'm almost always proven wrong by what the market says (how people vote).

For example, when I launched *How to NOT Suck at Writing Your First Book*, these were the three cover designs in the competition:

With this book, I was having trouble deciding what cover was best. I couldn't tell which one truly fit the message I was trying to send. However, my followers voted on the first one, so I went with it. And they proved correct. The book's doing really well, and so many people in my network were excited to play a part in the creation of the book. A real win-win!

And, as you likely know by now, the point of the competition isn't just to land the best cover. The point is to get people involved. To get feedback. To create a dialogue.

THE OTHER SIDE OF THE COIN

Walking hand in hand with our Building Buzz Strategy is the *Jab, Jab, Jab, Right Hook philosophy*. Contrary to its rough and tough name, you will discover that it entails a light touch, pairing perfectly with my tactful Building Buzz Strategy.

Gary Vaynerchuck introduced me to his *Jab, Jab, Jab, Right Hook philosophy* in his book that goes by the same name, *Jab, Jab, Jab, Right Hook*. Gary's concept is exactly what you and your launch team need to be doing when promoting your book.

In a nutshell, the *Jab, Jab, Jab, Right Hook* philosophy can be understood as—

Give, Give, Give, Ask.

In a world where we are surrounded by people asking us to do things for them, we need to be the needle in the haystack that gives instead of recieves. That is what is going to make you stand out in a sea of "askers." That way, when you do have to ask, you've done so much giving beforehand, that your "ask" is beyond acceptable. People will actually be clamoring to respond to your "ask."

For our book marketing purposes, we'll be using a modified version of the *Jab, Jab, Jab, Right Hook* philosophy—

Give, Give, Get people involved, Give—and then Ask.

Do not isolate yourself, instead share your author-hero's triumphs, challenges, and get people involved.

Sharing the milestones of your author-hero's writing journey is a way of giving and getting your audience involved, which is why the modified version of the Jab, Jab, Jab, Right Hook philosophy complements our Buzz Building Strategy so well. Both market your book tactfully and steadily.

You should be giving so much that when you do ask for help, people are eager to get involved.

BEST-SELLING AUTHOR TIP!

As you are building buzz for you book, include your launch team in the fun. You want to get them involved in everything you do while building buzz. They will multiply your reach tremendously.

Chapter 15

USING YOUR BOOK TO BUILD AN AUDIENCE (AND AN EMAIL LIST)

TO THE FRONT OF THE LINE—THE SUBSCRIBER LIST

While everyone is focused on social media marketing and how you need to be Periscoping, Snapchatting, Facebooking, and building up your "Like" page to gain an audience, I am going to show you how to be one step ahead of the game.

It's not that social media marketing is irrelevant. I like it, I use it, and it does make it easier to successfully launch a book. But it isn't a cure-all. Plus, it's really more of a distraction to buyers than anything else.

The good news is, there is a new way to build an audience. And that's through an email list.

While people go to social media to be entertained, they go to email to get things done. People go to email for a single purpose—to take action.

The email list is tried and true, and it's not going away. It's the universal communication medium nearly everyone uses.

Building a subscriber list through the use of your book is a much more advanced and strategic plan to meet your long-term goals. It is going to set you apart from the competition—forever.

Don't worry if you have no subscriber list or a very small one. An email list is not a mandatory factor in launching your book. But it will help you build an audience for your goals beyond launching a book.

So, if you don't have a following, an email list, or any idea about how to build one, what do you do? Should you build your email list before you launch your book so you will have audience? Or do you launch your book to build an email list?

With questions like these, you develop "chicken or the egg" syndrome. . .

THE OBVIOUS ANSWER

Just like the age-old chicken or egg question, the same can be applied to an email list. Which should come first—the audience or the book?

Some people say you need to build an audience, so you can market your book successfully. Others will tell you to launch a book first and that will bring an audience.

So which one is it?

The answer is obvious—*do the book first.*

The book is how you build an audience and authority. It's how you get people to listen to you, and it's the seed from which a dedicated audience sprouts.

Most people struggle when they have zero audience and zero list. They find themselves resorting to begging to try to get people to trust them, "Hey! Listen to me! I promise I'm smart and important and know more than you do about 'x.' "

People's response: "Prove it. Give me your credentials. Give me some kind of evidence, and then I might listen."

If you have a book, you *can* prove it. You're more established than ninety-nine percent of the population in their eyes, because they see the book as something very impressive, something they probably could never do.

They will think, "Hey, this guy's a best-selling author? He must be more knowledgeable on subject 'x' than I am, so I should listen to him. He has more influence, more knowledge."

So, I will show you how your book is going to build you that list, connecting you with readers for the long term.

THE HOLY GRAIL

The million dollar question: how do you turn book buyers into email subscribers?

The old-school way that authors tried to get readers to opt in to an email list was to litter their books with multiple opt-in links, pleading with readers to sign on—*Do you want more of this? Go to this site! If you want to know the final secret—go to this site and sign up!*

As you can imagine, this doesn't work well.

You should never give readers the impression you've given them *some* of your stuff, but if they want to learn it *all*, they have to go to your site, opt in to your email list, or pay more money. That's not fair to the book buyer. And it creates distrust between the reader and the writer.

Most authors don't resort to such hostile and annoying tactics to entice readers to opt in to subscriber lists. Instead, they place a call to action, giving readers the opportunity to opt in, at the end of their books. But the problem with placing the call to action at the end of the final chapter is—*less than twenty percent of people who buy a book actually finish reading it.*

So, knowing that, it doesn't make sense to place the call to action at the end of the book. I know this from firsthand experience. I did it with *The Productive Person*. We had five thousand-plus downloads during the first week of our launch, but barely any new subscribers to our email list.

We couldn't understand why those five thousands-plus downloads didn't result in at least two thousand opt-ins. Then we finally figured it out—we had our only call to action at the end of the book.

DANGLING THE GOLDEN CARROT

I learned two valuable lessons from the *The Productive Person* launch: (1) don't rely on the end of the book and (2) don't do an action guide.

What most authors do to land opt-ins (build their email lists) is offer free supplemental material that accompanies the book. This material may take the form of a PDF checklist, a condensed guide, a workbook, etc. In order to access this free material, the reader must give his or her email address (hence the opt-in) to which the free material is sent.

However, I learned with *The Productive Person* that, contrary to popular belief, action guides and free PDF's don't yield significant opt-in numbers.

Instead, here are the two best options for yielding high numbers of opt-ins:

Golden Carrot One—Video
Offer a video. The video may give people a behind-the-scenes tour, a course, a summary of the book, a backstory for a character or event, or even background information about you, the author. These are all things readers will enjoy. They will have no problem giving you their email addresses for this type of information because people appreciate exclusive, more in-depth material.

Golden Carrot Two—Audio (*My personal favorite)
Offer a free audio version of your book. Audiobooks add a TON of value to you and your readers. They give you the leg up on all the competition in so many different ways.

When a person finds a free audiobook giveaway offered in the opening of your book, they'll happily give you their email address in return for an audiobook they would have paid $8-$15 for elsewhere.

This situation gives a great example of Gary Vaynerchuck's *Give, Give, Give, Ask* marketing philosophy. An audiobook is a huge "give" to a reader, especially in comparison to the small "ask" the reader responds to in order to receive the audiobook. And for the author, getting a reader's email address is a huge score. The email address is the writer's way of creating a long-term relationship with readers, becoming the long-term audience member.

REVERBERATION BEYOND AMAZON

Audiobooks are great because they don't involve creating any more content. You can send the book to a professional voice actor, who will do your audiobook for anywhere between $300 and $400, or you can record it yourself.

So yes, you must invest some money and/or time in order to get your book made into an audiobook. However, know that later on, your audiobook will pay for itself and then some.

THE HOW AND WHERE ON THE OPT-IN

As far as placement goes, I recommend putting your opt-in page as early in the book as possible, within the first few pages.

This offers 2 benefits:

1. The maximum amount of people will see your giveaway/opt-in (meaning more subscribers).
2. People can give you their email address without buying the book.

The first benefit is self explanatory but I'll take a minute to explain the second.

Inside Amazon, on your book page there is a "Look Inside" feature that allows readers to preview the first 10% of your book before purchase.

If your opt-in page is within the first few pages, they can see it, click over to your site, and opt-in!

This is exactly what I do for most of my books, and it captures thousands of leads for my business (check it out to see exactly what I mean): http://self-publishingschool.com/writing-book

When people find the free audiobook via the "Look Inside" feature, readers will probably think they've put one over on you, the author. But the thing is, you will have collected their email addresses, which is typically much more valuable than more book sales.

Now you have the power to further communicate and make offers to that person through email. Two weeks later, when you send customers an email introducing your high-end product or service, they'll be much more likely to take you up on your offer.

Using this method, my recent book "Book Launch" brought in 3,334 leads and $92,228.50 in backend revenue within fifty-five days after the book was released, all from investing a few hundred dollars into an audiobook.

NO PRODUCTS OR SERVICES BEYOND YOUR BOOK, THEN WHAT?

Even if you have no other business, no other site, or no other products or services that your book feeds into, I still recommend that you capture as many opt-ins as you can with your book.

Why? For starters, you may end up writing a second book or a series of books, so you'll want your readers' email addresses to continue communicating with them.

This is the position R.E. Vance found himself in. R.E. always dreamed of being a full-time writer of urban fantasy stories. For him, his first book wouldn't guide readers toward his business. Instead, he needed to build a large, loyal audience of readers that would seek out his future books.

In advancing through the SPS 90-Day Way, when R.E. reached this point, he immediately realized the outstanding opportunity in building an email list. In this way, R.E. has been building a large and engaged audience of readers for his book series, *Paradise Lot*.

THE TEMPLATES

Since an email list is so important, I want to make sure you use the optimal language and images on your "opt-in page." Below are two different opt-in pages I use, one that offers an audiobook and the other, a video course. Feel free to use these as templates when creating your own.

Now that you know how to build an audience using your book, it's time to learn how to successfully launch your book.

Following the SPS 90-Day way, we've almost arrived at launch week. So, it's time for us to address launch-day strategies.

In the coming chapters, I'll present four approaches to book launching, giving you detailed characteristics and implementation steps for each, so you and your team can decide the approach that best meets your situation and long-term plans.

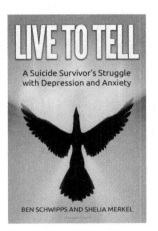

INSPIRATIONAL INTERLUDE

Shelia Merkel got the idea to co-write a book with Ben Schwipps when she visited him in the hospital shortly after his second suicide attempt. It was a sheer miracle that he survived the gunshot wound to the head, and Shelia knew for certain that Ben was alive for a reason and that his story needed to be told.

Also, Shelia admits, "I was desperate to give him something to live for. I thought that writing would be therapeutic." For Shelia, writing a book had always been a distant dream, so she knew she was the person that could help him do it.

In their book, *Live to Tell*, Ben shares what was going on in his life and his mind that led to him attempting to kill himself. In sharing the raw and unsettling details from this time in his life, as well as well-researched facts and advice about depression and suicide, Shelia and Ben hope to save at least one life. Shelia explains *Live to Tell*'s big message: as:

> If you are a depressed individual, please know that you are not alone in your fight. There are answers, and people want to help you. On the flip side, we also need to take more risks and show more compassion to those who are struggling. We are not alone in this world for a reason. We want readers to take action and reach out and connect with someone, as you never know who is struggling and who is at the end of their rope . . . literally.

When I asked Shelia if *Live to Tell* made the difference they'd hoped for, she responded:

It is doing amazing with minimal promotion. The reviews are compelling and very humbling, all five-star ratings, thirty-one reviews within three days, and #1 status achieved in the "free" store...within three days of launch. The book is having a broader reach and impact than we both expected.

People are literally coming out of the woodwork wanting to connect and talk about someone they care about who is struggling, or readers just want to relay their own personal stories. One reader mentioned that she no longer carried the burden of being angry at her brother for killing himself. She felt more at peace now that she better understood what her brother was dealing with.

This book has opened a new window to give people permission to talk about the dark, forbidden topics of depression and suicide.

Honestly, I don't see how Ben and Shelia could have hoped for a better response. But it does get better because the sharing of his story has contributed positively to Ben's recovery too:

For Ben, putting his story on paper has been like therapy. Ben now sees new opportunities to get involved with church groups or with depression support groups in the future to share his story and offer support to others who need a helping hand. We both feel a sense of accomplishment from writing a book.

And for Shelia:

For me, I feel more confident to take on new challenges. Writing other books on subjects I am passionate about is no longer an out-of-reach dream.

Ben's bravery combined with Shelia's loving support worked to transform his distressing and horrific bout with depression and suicide into something valuable—a book.

A book provides purpose, worth, and direction to our pain because it opens it up, it shares it with others, which frees the writer and, at the same time, provides connection and support to readers who may be similarly suffering and alone.

Choose to connect with others. Commit to writing a book.

Section 4

LAUNCH WEEK

Chapter 16

PREP FOR LAUNCH: YOUR OPTIONS

LAUSANNE, SWITZERLAND

Allow me to set the scene: standing in the garden, we can just see Lake Geneva over the hedge. And beyond the lake, the mighty Alps stand in all their majesty. The air is a bit crisp, but it's early summer, so it will only get warmer as the day progresses.

The reason for our visit is to discuss with Vilfredo Pareto, the 1896 Italian economist, the best strategy for launching the book we've just written. Strangely, he insists upon showing us his peas. So that's why we're traversing the garden—to visit some peas.

At the pea patch, Dr. Pareto leans over excitedly to pluck off a pod, which he immediately pops open to expose ten perfect peas. The doctor quickly plucks a pod off a neighboring vine, pops it open, and reveals eight perfect peas. He pauses as if for emphasis. Admittedly, we're confused. We don't get what's happening, but if this is what we have to endure for him to share some sage advice, we're up for it.

From here, Dr. Pareto moves to the other side of the patch, plucking pods off the vine as he goes. He must have grabbed twenty pods on this short jaunt. He motions us over to sit on the ground next to him.

Together, we open the pods to look at the peas. We're not finding much.

Out of four pods, we retrieved only about eight peas. In the end, from the twenty pods we only got about eighty-five peas. We'd been expecting almost two hundred. Weird.

We get up, and Dr. Pareto leads us back through the garden, into the house, and to the front door. He opens the door, saying something in Italian that we don't quite catch.

Luckily, we've got Siri with us to help translate. Siri tells us that Dr. Pareto said, "Use the pea numbers to launch your book."

What?

PARETO AND YOUR BOOK LAUNCH

Here's the deal. Dr. Pareto is the man who, from observing the peas in his garden, formulated the Pareto Principle, a.k.a. the "80/20 Rule." Pareto determined that 80% of the new peas in his garden came from only 20% of the peapods. From this, he presumed that 80 to 20 could be a special ratio.

Then he looked at landownership and found this same ratio playing out—approximately 80% of the land in Italy was owned by 20% of the Italian population.

This ratio plays out in commerce in that about 80% of a business' sales occur from just 20% of its buyers. In terms of time management, the Pareto Principle shows that 80% of your results come from how you spend just 20% of your time.

The 80/20 Rule, in essence, is a further championing of the rifle approach for marketing your book. It is another argument to concentrate your marketing efforts on specific people, i.e., your target audience, because those people will more than amply reward you. Your target audience is your twenty peapods that will give you the most peas.

With the 80/20 Rule at its core, take this statement to heart: less is more when it comes to launching a book. You will make the most gains by focusing on the people and things that move the needle. You already know who the people are, your ideal readers, so the trick is determining the "few things" you need to do on your end during launch week.

BACK TO THE DRAWING BOARD: REVISITING YOUR PURPOSE

When it comes time to launch your book and decide which of my four launch strategies (in the coming chapters) is the one for you, the first thing you need to do is think all the way back to the original purpose behind your book. Take a moment and revisit *your* purpose. This is the time to drill down and really think about *why* you are doing this.

Is your purpose a passion project? A glorified business card? An authority piece? A book to generate leads? To grow your business? To share an important story? A combination of two of these?

Let's use the example of generating leads for your business. If that is a primary reason why you are launching your book, then you will want to give away as many copies of the book as you possibly can.

There are other, more effective ways to make money than to monetize a $2.99 ebook. That's why I don't mind giving my books away for free—because every copy that I give away is another lead for my business. (This works for my situation, but it doesn't mean it will be a perfect fit for yours. I'll be going into this more later on.)

And instead of making less than three dollars selling my book, I'm getting the opportunity to legitimize my business (through the book's content) and then sell my larger product, Self-Publishing School (SPS). The single customer that buys SPS supplies me with much greater revenue than that of an individual Kindle consumer.

With a strategy like this, your book becomes more than a way to make a profit; it becomes a lead source.

Your purpose for writing your book, and some other factors, will determine which of the four following launch strategies will be the best one for you to choose.

THE FOUR MAJOR LAUNCH STRATEGIES

To launch your book, I will present to you four strategies to choose from. It is up to you to decide the one that will work best for your needs. Please, keep in mind Pareto's Principle, the rifle approach to marketing, and our version of the Jab, *Jab, Jab, Right Hook* marketing philosophy when deciding the strategy that best fits your long-term goals.

Along with the explanation of each launch strategy, I'll offer weighty opinions on who I think should use each strategy, the pros and cons of each, as well as implementation steps for each one.

Here are the four launch strategies:

The Free Launch (Amazon Launch)

The $0.99 Launch (Amazon Launch)

The Traditional Launch

The Free-Plus Shipping Launch

Understand, there is some ambiguity in choosing a launch plan; there isn't one perfect plan for everyone out there. However, if you do not have a strong purpose or longer-term goal behind your book, by the time you start implementing this information, it is going to be extremely difficult to choose the most fitting launch strategy. Everything comes full circle. Everything stems from the purpose, so you must be deliberate in determining yours.

Also, the first two strategies (Free Launch and $0.99 Launch) are for people who are self-publishing, first time authors, or who don't have an audience.

The second two methods (Traditional Launch and Free-Plus Shipping Hard Copy Launch) are for those of you that want to go with a publisher and/or have a huge following.

I don't want the second two strategies to intimidate you, but they are for the advanced. I have decided to include them in the book because they will give you great marketing advice that you can use on top of what you have found in the first two methods, which will benefit you in the long run.

Again, no matter what launch plan you choose, you are still going to build buzz and work with a hand-picked launch team. Everything I have recommended to you previously still applies.

This is where the rubber meets the road. And these launch strategies are like four different roads leading to four major cities. You just might take a different car than someone else, but let me caution you: do not try to make a hybrid path by combining various strategies. If you do, the only place you'll get to is Nowheresville. Split focus yields split results.

Once you encounter the four launch strategies, you have to make a choice. I am responsible for guiding you to the choice. You are responsible for owning it.

Without further ado, let's jump into the first launch strategy.

Chapter 17

THE FREE LAUNCH STRATEGY

With the first book I ever launched, *The Productive Person*, I used the Free Launch Strategy. As you know, it is still successful today.

In launching *The Productive Person*, James and I did not have a following, we had no reputation, and we were just starting to build our brand. We were the epitome of "first-time authors."

We had to figure out this strategy (and all of them) as we went along. We learned from our mistakes, and, over time, we developed the Free Launch Strategy, specifically for beginning authors.

This method, and each of the following methods, are not theory. I built them because I have used them myself. I know what really works, and I know it will work for you too.

The Free Launch Strategy for launching a book is the most universal of all the strategies. It can work for nearly anyone and makes it easier to top the Amazon best-seller charts.

Who Is the Free Launch Strategy For?

o   The first-time author

o   An author without a huge following looking to build one

o   Someone looking to build momentum

o   Someone looking to establish a brand

o   An author with aspirations beyond book sales, such as a passion project, generating leads for your business, or establishing yourself as an expert

This is for people who want to get a lot of downloads and a lot of books out the door, especially if they don't already have a huge following.

Also, if being a best-selling author is your end goal, free charts are a lot easier to get to the top of than the paid charts . . . and your momentum on the free charts will draw such positive attention to your book that it will boost your success in the paid charts as well. When this happens, I call it the "whirlwind of wow," and I'll explain it in more detail soon.

However, because you probably have aspirations beyond books sales, the publicity you get at the top of the free charts will likely help you achieve your long-term goals.

Pros

o   Helps you get your book off the ground without having a huge following

o   Builds the greatest amount of buzz during your book launch (including maximum reviews and downloads)

o   Great for first-time authors with no audience

o   Easier to create great momentum and reach the maximum amount of people

o   Inspires people to download your book simply because it's free, and even more so, when it's also at the top of the charts and free

TEN THOUSAND GALLONS OF JUICE, PLEASE

Amazon chooses to promote certain products within its site and beyond. When an Amazon product is steeped in certain kinds of activity, Amazon will take it upon itself to promote the product within its site (see picture below). I call this free, organic Amazon promotion, the "Amazon juice."

While the precise characteristics Amazon draws on for deciding which products to promote are secret, I know that the greater the number of positive reviews you get and the more downloads you accumulate, then the more likely Amazon will apply its juice to your book.

A WHIRLWIND OF WOW!

The Free Launch Strategy capitalizes on Amazon's juicing of certain products. Because your book is free, you are more likely to get many downloads, thus many reviews, both of which drive your book to the top of the free charts and simultaneously lead to free promotion by Amazon, i.e., the juice. All of which, in turn, leads to more downloads, more reviews, thus a higher and more established place at the top of the charts and even more Amazon juice, which then leads to even more.

In the picture below, you can see that Amazon featured our book, *The Productive Person*, in three different spots just on one page—that's some serious Amazon juice!

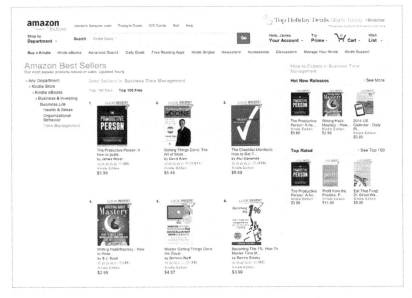

Now, it's time to share the flipside, the cons.

Cons

o   "Free" people are not dependable readers.

o   You can't rely on as many "free" people to opt in to your other offers as people who paid even a very small fee for your book.

o   It cannibalizes a small amount of sales that would've paid for the book.

IMPLEMENTATION PLAN

If the Free Launch Strategy fits the purpose of your book and your long-term goals, the remainder of this chapter consists of a step-by-step launch plan that I guarantee will work for you.

Step 1: Upload Your Book

It's imperative that you upload your book three to five days before your launch day. Not sooner. Not later.

BEST-SELLING AUTHOR TIP!

Since you are waiting until three to five days before the launch of your book to upload it, you will want to make sure your book is formatted (in a MOBI or ePUB file) correctly at least a week or two before you upload.

To do this, use Kindle Previewer one week before launch to make sure everything looks good and is formatted correctly.

If you are having difficulty with the formatting, you can also find freelancers who specialize in formatting ebooks. Just look on freelancing sites like Upwork.

Step 2: The Free Promo

When you upload your book, set it at an inflated price of $4.99-$9.99. This will be the price to keep during the length of the "Free Promo," which I'll explain in detail shortly.

Kindle does a great job of marketing for you. When the "Free Promo" is on, they strikethrough the price and report, "You save $9.99" (or whatever the price you set for the book is).

The higher the listing price, the higher the perceived value of the giveaway during your promo. But just to keep your promo legitimized, I don't recommend going above $9.99 during this stage of promotion.

Here is a picture to show you what it looks like on your book page. It's pretty awesome and does a lot to boost sales.

Digital List Price: $9.99 What's this? ⌄
Kindle Price: $0.00
You Save: $9.99 (100%)

Step 3: Launch Day

I get this question all the time:

What day of the week should I launch my book?

Traditionally, book launches and music album releases are on Tuesdays.

Book publishers and record labels figured out long ago that Tuesday is the best day to launch because it's the day after Monday, so, for most people, this means the craziness of starting the week has somewhat died down. You can get people's attention on Tuesday and market to them all the way up until they escape into the weekend.

BEST-SELLING AUTHOR TIP!
Taking this a step farther, if you are planning to launch your book around a holiday, don't be scared. Surprisingly, it does not affect your sales enough to delay your launch until after the holiday. So don't push your launch back for anything, especially a holiday!

While you have the option to do a full five-day free promo, starting on a Tuesday, I do not recommend it. In my experience working with hundreds of writers through SPS, I've found that the full five-day "free promo" is not ideal.

From doing tests on many book launches, I've developed the single **best strategy** for you to employ:

○ Launch your book on a Tuesday.

○ Schedule within Amazon that you are doing a five-day free promo.

○ Advertise to your following that your book is available for free for only two or three days (as in, don't share that it is available for free for the full five days).

With this strategy, you have the benefits of launching on a Tuesday, but with a tightly focused "free promo" time, thus creating a higher sense of urgency for people in your following and beyond to download your book while it's free.

While Amazon will allow you to schedule your "free promo" for two or three days, as you just read, I recommend scheduling it for the full five days (and only advertising it as available for two or three days) just to have that cushion of extra days in case you need it.

If you achieve the high number of downloads you wanted in those two or three days, then you can halt the scheduled five-day "free promo" at that point. If you haven't achieved the number of downloads you hoped for, you can continue the "free promo" after the two or three days, using all five of the scheduled days.

IMPORTANT!

No matter when you choose to start your promo, always advertise that your book will be free for a shorter amount of time than the amount of time that it actually will be. Then, it will be a pleasant surprise if/when you decide to extend the promo.

BEST-SELLING AUTHOR TIP!

Make sure to schedule your promo (inside Kindle Direct Publishing (KDP)) at least twenty-four hours before you want it to start. If not, you will have to wait one more day for the promo to be activated.

Also, don't forget about using your launch team here. This is what they are for! Even if you already gave them a free PDF of your book, you are still going to want to keep them posted on your launch. Definitely ask your launch team members to download and review your book during this time.

Step 4: Book Marketing for Launch Week

This is what all the delicate, subtle marketing you'll be trickling out to your following over the course of the ninety days will be leading to.

In week one, you'll have alerted your following that you have started your author-hero's journey. You share when you've written the fifth chapter, then the tenth. You'll send out a photo of yourself with a massive grin when you finish the first draft. Your following will know how nervous you are to send the book off to an editor. Eight weeks in you'll engage your following in a cover competition that results in chatter and debate. So many people you haven't heard from directly will write and congratulate you when you announce it's time for launch day.

Over the course of the three months, you will do a lot of sharing and a lot of giving, building anticipation for this very launch. Your following will be ready to act. All you have to do is ask. In Chapter Twenty-one, I'll share with you my approach for "asking" your following to do their part.

When your following does their part, downloading your book and writing positive reviews, they are positioning your book so that Amazon will take notice of it and give it that Amazon juice, which in turn should get that "whirlwind of wow" spinning.

Even though you don't make any direct money during the free download period, your success during this time leads to making even more money when your book changes to "paid" because of the "Amazon juice" your book will have acquired.

Step 5: Switching to Paid

When it is time to switch your book to "paid," the starting paid price should be at $0.99 for one week. You will bump up the price one dollar per week until you hit your sweet spot in sales. Or, if you have a pretty good idea of where that sweet spot will be, you can jump straight to that desired price after the seven $0.99 days. Keep an eye on the best-selling charts and watch how high you soar!

And there you have it—The Free Launch Strategy. Yes, there are a lot of moving parts, but if you take it one step at a time, you will be able to keep everything under control, working it to your benefit.

Let me repeat: I especially recommend this strategy for every first-time author out there. You can easily reach #1 in your particular Amazon category, your book becomes a bestseller, and you get wins under your belt. That's my whole aim—for you, first-time authors, to get those wins!

Arturo Nava, author of *Logra Tu Dream*, had major success with this launch strategy, achieving each of the wins mentioned above.

His book made it to number one in *six categories* in both the free and paid store. To top off his success, in his launch week alone, his book garnered fifty-six positive reviews, giving him the "Amazon juice" to have long-lasting success.

When you reach this point, you really should have something to celebrate. You should feel accomplished. You're getting your message out there, building authority, and well on the road to achieving those long-term goals. You should be proud of that.

In the next chapter, I reveal the $0.99 Launch Strategy. You'll find it similar to the Free Launch Strategy, just a little more involved

INSPIRATIONAL INTERLUDE

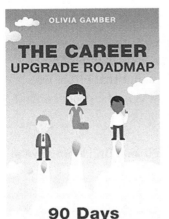

OLIVIA GAMBER

THE CAREER
UPGRADE ROADMAP

90 Days
to a Better Job and a Better Life

First-time writer Olivia Gamber explained that the big message of her book *The Career Upgrade Roadmap* is to help readers "understand that there are new rules to the game of career advancement, and you don't have to wait for an opportunity to come, but you can go out there and create your own, using [my 'career upgrade'] process."

For those of you with busy lives, wondering when you can possibly find the time to write a book (and market and publish it), Olivia confirms what I've been telling you, "[The SPS 90-Day Way] process outline allowed me to write and publish a book in ninety days with a demanding corporate job. I can't say I would have done this otherwise."

To determine which of the four strategies to implement for her book launch, Olivia returned to her original purpose for writing the book—to establish herself as an expert in the career development space and attract more high quality leads to her web-based business. The Free Launch Strategy was the obvious choice, and Olivia is ecstatic about the results:

> I did a three-day "free promo" and received a little over 2,300 downloads. I did this because my book was created in order to build credibility and grow my email list. My email list was just over 100 people before my book, now it is at 370. The book has more than tripled my email list. I have gotten coaching clients and customers from these leads. If you can find a way to use your book to build leads, it can be profitable faster.

Once my book moved to "paid," I sold 267 Kindle versions and 47 paperbacks from December 6 to December 31 [of 2015]. My total royalties for [December] will be around $400.

I am still getting on average five leads per day from my book, [people] that sign up to my email list through either my free workbook or my free video series. These are people I am able to offer my products and services to.

While the success Olivia has achieved is great, it isn't unbelievable or shocking. Why? Because Olivia's winning results are exactly what I designed the SPS 90-Day Way to deliver. Yes, Olivia had to put in a lot of effort during the course of the ninety days, but that effort was focused and organized according to where she was in the process. And her bonanza-like results—another part of the plan too.

When you commit to the SPS 90-Day Way, you'll also find a bonanza at the end of the journey, just wait and see!

Chapter 18

$0.99 LAUNCH STRATEGY

If you are the kind of person who really can't stand the thought of giving your book away for free, the good news is . . .

You don't have to.

We have arrived at the second launch strategy—the $0.99 Launch.

I launched my fifth book, *How to Not SUCK at Writing Your First Book*, following this exact method. While I'd developed the $0.99 Launch Strategy long before publishing my fifth book, to keep myself up-to-date with what I was teaching, I "took my own medicine" and applied the strategy to my launch.

At that point in my career, I was much more of an established author than when I'd launched *The Productive Person*, my first published book. At the launching of my fifth book, I had already grounded myself as an authority in my niche.

Using the $0.99 Launch Strategy, *How to Not SUCK at Writing Your First Book* successfully reached the top of its Amazon categories and, just like The Productive Person, is still doing well today.

Who Is the $0.99 Launch Strategy For?

o   People already "established" in their niches or fields, and looking for more leads

o   Those thinking a free launch will devalue their existing brands

- o Those with email lists of at least 500 to 1,000 people looking to expand
- o People with existing followings
- o Those writing passion projects with major organizations backing their launches

If climbing the paid charts and making your book extremely visible is where your focus is and you have the following to back it up, I highly recommend giving this launch plan a shot.

However, as previously mentioned, it is much harder to get to the top of the paid charts than it is the free charts, so without the "Amazon juice" you can readily get from a free launch, it will be more difficult to climb to the top without support from a significant amount of people.

If you think you can make your own "Amazon juice" with your following, then the $0.99 launch is going to fit perfectly with your book.

Pros

- o This launch plan gives your book greater longevity in the paid store.
- o You get book royalties from the start of your launch.
- o It creates a sense of urgency to buy the book before the price increases.

If you can pull off this launch the right way, your book will often times stay at the top of the paid charts longer than it would if you were launching your book for "free." Thus, more people are going to see it, buy it, and read it! In turn, this should result in your already extensive following growing even larger.

Cons

- o In comparison to the Free Launch, you'll get less downloads and exposure upfront— meaning fewer leads and less people impacted.
- o You are taking more of a gamble with climbing the charts.

Since you are already familiar with the Free Launch, understanding the $0.99 Launch should be a breeze. They basically run the exact same way, *except* you do not tell your following when the book will be available for free. For the two or three days you run the free promo, you will drive different traffic to your book, getting the Amazon juice you need. When your book changes from "free" to $0.99, you will then announce your launch.

You will market the book the same as you would with the Free Launch, but, to reiterate, you only start broadcasting your book's launch to your following once it is available for $0.99.

You will leave your book at $0.99 for one week and bump up the price one dollar per week until you hit your sweet spot in sales. Or, if you have a pretty good idea of where that sweet spot will be, you can jump straight to that desired price after the seven $0.99 days.

In essence, the $0.99 Launch is a middle ground between the Free Launch and the Traditional Launch (presented in the next chapter). The main difference is the schedule you need to make for your launch and the large following you've already acquired.

IMPLEMENTATION PLAN

Let's carefully review the steps involved in this launch strategy.

Step 1: Upload Your Book

The first thing you need to do is upload your book on the Tuesday before it launches. This will give you enough time to fix any errors and deal with any unwarrented surprises.

Step 2: Schedule Your Promo

You are going to schedule three days of "free promo" within the Amazon system. Make sure that these three days occur on a Saturday, Sunday, and Monday.

You are not going to share with your large following that your book is available for free for these three days. However, you will inform those in your very closest circle, your family and friends, and ask them to download it, read it, and write a review. Even if they already have a PDF copy of your book, explain to them that Amazon rewards your book for the number of downloads and positive reviews it gets, so it would really help you if they downloaded it from Amazon Kindle too.

Also, you will do a web search for "free book promotion websites" and submit your book and its days of "free promo" to the sites. These sites will send traffic to your book, thus resulting in more downloads and reviews.

The reason for having the "secret" days when your book is available free of charge is to get a little bit of "Amazon juice" going on your book before your large following works its magic. You are aiming for around 1,000+ downloads and as many reviews as possible during these three "secret" days of "free promo." I call this your "stealth launch" before your real launch day.

Step 3: Stop the Promo!
Before you know it, the Tuesday of your $0.99 launch day will arrive.

You will need to manually stop the "free promo" between 12:00 p.m. and 3:00 p.m. the day before your $0.99 launch. This will give Amazon plenty of time to process the changes you've made to your book to ensure it is $0.99 as you've promised.

Step 4: The BIG ASK
You and your launch team will then proceed with the BIG ASK. You will notify your email list and social media followers that your book is out. You will leverage your launch team and their personal networks too.

The trick is to time everything right. You want your large following to hit the book in a single forty-eight hour period. Think of it like this: you start by holding the dam to allow the water to build up. Then, on launch day, you let the dam break. The rush of activity will shoot your book to the top of the charts.

So, don't let the cat out of the bag before the book is at $0.99.

Avery Breyer, author of *How to Raise Your Credit Score*, had major success with the $0.99 Launch. She was already established in her niche and knew she was equipped enough to bypass the Free Launch.

Even still, Avery admits that it can be a little nerve-wracking relying on your following to push your book to success.

Her following came through for her in sweeping numbers, buying her book at $0.99 and writing positive reviews, so much so that *How to Raise Your Credit Score* reached the number one position in two categories on Amazon.

Avery's success story is a great reminder that for those who already have a dependable and large following, the $0.99 Launch Strategy can yield tremendous rewards.

Read on to learn about the final two advanced launch strategies before deciding which one makes the most sense for you.

Chapter 19

THE TRADITIONAL LAUNCH STRATEGY

Chances are, if you have seen a traditional book launch from a big name author, the author followed this method.

For decades, all authors published their books using the Traditional Launch Strategy because it was the proven path to success. Although it relies on traditional media, antiquated marketing tactics, and requires a lot of work, it has become the standard.

This is very much an "old school" strategy and brings to light out of date methods, but don't be afraid to use the methods if you see value in them for your particular situation.

Because of its notoriety and longevity in the marketplace, the Traditional Launch Strategy is often the first choice for many first-time authors.

However, the Traditional Launch Strategy is actually the least effective for beginners to employ because it requires the writer to have a large and existing audience to get the needed traction for the strategy to work.

Also, being signed with a publisher is almost a necessity for this strategy to be a success. The only way to get around a big name publisher is having a HUGE brand or following. But, in saying that, this is the strategy where publishers will come to your rescue the most.

The Traditional Launch Strategy requires you to "get your foot in the door" with as many big name people, influencers, and publications in your field as possible. With a publisher, it is much easier to get in those doors because they are already opened for you.

I would not recommend this strategy to ninety-nine percent of the people reading this book, because I am a self-publishing advocate, and because this is one of the least effective launch strategies.

Even if you decide not to choose the Traditional Launch Strategy, pay close attention to this chapter because some of the methods included below can be adapted and "layered" (but be careful-- don't make a hybrid method!) on top of either one of the first two launch strategies.

Who Is the Traditional Launch For?

o   People publishing hard copies with a major publisher

o   Public speakers, consultants, or business owners

o   Those adept and experienced with gaining newspaper, radio show, or TV interviews

o   Authors who have published other books previously

o   Those willing to travel to promote their books

o   Authors who have a lot of time and money to invest in their book

If you have an audience, don't mind the travel and extra leg work, and want to do a hard-copy launch, the Traditional Launch Strategy is right for you! (Please note though that this is not a strategy I recommend for a self-published ebook.)

Pros

o   Allows for more mainstream media and attention for you and your book (especially helpful if you're a speaker, consultant, or if you run a personality-based business)

o   Creates a bigger boom for you, your business, and your backend products/services

o   Makes up for the lost money paid up front with backend product sales and increased business

Cons

o   Requires the largest time commitment out of all of the launch strategies

o   Is the most costly of all the strategies

o   Inefficient book marketing strategies, but better for gaining publicity

o   Moves less books with more effort (your effort per book sold is much higher due to inefficient marketing tactics)

o   Focuses on advertising your book on traditional media outlets rather than the internet

While this method has its ups and downs just like any of the methods out there, it puts you in a spot to achieve greatness—*if* you do it correctly.

BEST-SELLING AUTHOR TIP!

If you are considering this method, get a publisher. Before you waste your time, let me just say this: if you are self-publishing, do not use this strategy.

IMPLEMENTATION GUIDE

Rather than giving you a step-by-step launch *plan* I decided to give you a *guide* to follow instead. This marketing guide will consist of different tasks that you, as the author, will need to choose from when marketing and launching your book.

But keep in mind: marketing with this strategy is anything but "the road less travelled." There is a reason why I named this strategy "traditional."

With the Traditional Launch, the real leg work happens before your book comes out. Your number one goal is to get the attention of as many media outlets as possible.

You will want to appear in a multitude of newspapers, magazines, TV shows, and radio shows (and other speaking engagements). It's a good idea to snail mail letters, postcards, and even a copy of the book to influencers you think would be interested.

You will launch your book similarly as in the Free and $0.99 Launch Strategies. Except, you will not run any free promotions of any kind. You will shift your marketing focus to other mediums, mainly focusing on your hard copy book.

You will want to launch your book on a Tuesday and price it at the standard price, between $2.99 and $3.99 for your ebook version and $11.99 to $15.99 for a hard copy.

Task 1: The Party
You will want to kick off your launch with the biggest and best book launch party you can think of (yes, an actual party with food, friends, and family).

If you are concerned with getting book reviews, you can ask people to read and review your book at the party.

If you are concerned with moving your hard copy books, you can have them for sale at your party or you can include them in a gift bag given to party guests.

If you choose to give the book away as a gift, understand that you will have to cover the cost up front and order the books. You can easily make your money back by having your guests pay a $15-$25 admission fee to attend your party, thus covering the cost of the gift bag.

Task 2: Book Signings
You will immediately follow your launch with book signings across your state or country. No, you will probably not sell a ton of books during these events, but it does give you the opportunity to introduce your name to people that might not have seen it before now.

Think about it: people buy your book at the event, you spend a couple hours signing your name and taking a few pictures and you've not only gotten publicity, but sold some books along the way.

Task 3: The Book Tour

This is probably the most beneficial task for moving books. It's a more modern technique, but it has the same principles as a book signing.

Much like a band would go on tour for their newest album, you are going to go on tour for your book.

When you do a book tour, you are going to have people host an event for you in various cities around your country (or around the world if you're ambitious). The hosts will aid you in advertising for this book tour and be responsible for coordinating the event.

At the event, you will give a speech or do some kind of activity with the people who come to your event.

Again, you may give your book away for free and have a cover fee for the event or simply have the books for sale at a table.

BEST-SELLING AUTHOR TIP!

Remember when I taught you about having a launch team? With this strategy, now is the time to bring them back into play. Have the members of your launch team host your events in the cities they live in.

Task 4: Speeches

Giving speeches goes hand and hand with your book tour. While you are planning for the events, you will want to allot time for a speech by you, the author. People would not be at the event if they were not interested in meeting you or seeing you speak.

Just like people do not go to rock concerts to listen to a recording of the band's songs.

With this type of book marketing, it is also common to do a speaking gig in return for the event coordinator making bulk purchases of your book to give to everyone in attendance.

Task 5: Getting Featured

It's important to aim for TV interviews, as well as newspaper and magazine feature articles and interviews.

Getting featured in major media outlets will give you the opportunity to reach an audience that you normally would not be able to reach while also giving you more exposure and credibility.

Task 6: Giveaways

It also is a good idea to employ the traditional book giveaways. These are bonuses you give people for purchasing more than one copy of your book.

These bonuses/giveaways should make it a no-brainer for people to buy more than just one copy.

Here are some bonus examples to get you thinking:

- "Buy five books, get a signed copy free!"
- "Buy 10 books, get a recording of my latest webinar free!"
- "Buy my course and get a signed copy of my book for free!"
- "Buy 1,000 copies and I'll come speak at your conference or seminar."

BEST-SELLING AUTHOR TIP!

Your book tour, interviews, giveaways, etc., should happen during your launch week. Keep that book launch party going!

Unlike the other strategies, the Traditional Launch Strategy boils down to this: if it's a tried-and-true, classic marketing technique, you want to go for it.

But, on top of all the traditional marketing strategies, in today's new age, it makes perfect sense to tap into new media outlets as well.

By simultaneously tapping into both new and traditional media, you will be doubling the exposure for your book, thus doubling your audience and potential buyers.

The following "tasks" are the top options I recommend for new media outlets while employing this launch strategy.

Task 7: Blogs and Podcasts

Just as it is important to be in newspapers and radio shows, it is also important to be featured on blogs and podcasts, especially the established ones.

This will also allow you to reach a younger audience, who may be more interested in your book to begin with.

Here's what Hal Elrod, author of *The Miracle Morning*, has to say about the ability of podcasts to move books:

> "Having just surpassed 100,000 copies sold (and with over 1,000+ 5-star reviews) for my self-published book, *The Miracle Morning: The Not-So-Obvious Secret Guaranteed to Transform Your Life* (Before 8AM), I can confidently say that the number one key to driving book sales has been securing interviews on other people's podcasts!

> It used to be TV shows that you wanted to get on to sell books. However, not only are podcasts now proving to sell more books than TV, they're free to get booked on! I invested over $10,000 to get myself booked on 15 local and national TV shows (and saw very little increase in sales) and then invested zero dollars to get booked on over 200 podcasts, which has driven my sales to as high as 10,900+ copies in a single month.

A great place to start is to look on iTunes in the 'New and Noteworthy' section to find podcasters who are new (so they're not inundated with requests) but are gaining a lot of momentum and listeners. Google them, go to their websites, and reach out to tell them how you and your book would add extraordinary value for their audiences!"

Task 8: Send Pre-Release Copies to Influencers

Frankly, this step comes way before step one, but it's such a powerful one, I opted to do the ol' save-the-best-for-last move. Here it goes . . .

What really puts the icing on the cake with this launch plan is sending pre-release copies of your book to as many influential people as possible before you officially launch your book.

In doing this, you have the option to:

o   ask for testimonials ahead of time (leveraging any influence you can get)

o   schedule even more podcast interviews and guest posts

o   get people to bulk buy your books in exchange for having you do a speaking event

BEST-SELLING AUTHOR TIP!

You will want to start pre-selling your book about ninety days before launch week (or earlier), even if you haven't technically finished your book.

You must also be very detailed when it comes to scheduling the marketing for this book. All of the promotions you use for your book must be strategically timed to blast off during launch week, the first week your book is officially available for purchase.

In the next chapter, you'll find the final strategy, the Free-Plus Shipping Launch Strategy. However, before you jump into it, let me warn you:

I only recommend this strategy to advanced marketers and experienced business people. If that's not you, feel free to move on to Chapter Twenty-one.

But if you choose to read it, even if you don't have an audience and don't plan to use this launch strategy, pay close attention to the promotional tactics in this chapter. They will give you insight into the world of marketing that might come in handy for you later down the road.

Chapter 20

FREE-PLUS SHIPPING LAUNCH STRATEGY

So far we have covered fairly straightforward ways to market and launch your book. However, the Free-Plus Shipping Launch Strategy is quite different because it's much more sophisticated and employs high-level direct-marketing tactics.

Out of all of the launch strategies, this is definitely the most difficult to implement. This launch strategy is not something everyone can use. In fact, it's probably only right for less than one percent of people reading this book. I recommend that only advanced marketers and/or experienced business people attempt to implement the Free-Plus Shipping Launch Strategy.

If you aren't one of those people (or if you don't love reading about marketing), you can skip this chapter and move on to Chapter Twenty-one.

If you choose to read this chapter (even if you are not able to implement it), it will still give you a deeper insight into the psychology of marketing and how to sell more books.

Who Is the Free-Plus Shipping Launch For?

o   Advanced and experienced marketers and business people

o   Business owners looking to acquire more paying customers

o   Online marketers who would like another acquisition funnel/way to acquire customers

o   Those who have websites where they sell other products and services

The Free-Plus Shipping Launch is all about turning subscribers, fans, or even strangers into paying customers. In this case, you do that by giving them a book for free, and all they have to do is pay for shipping and handling.

This is a great method for bringing in new customers because after they've given you their credit card information and paid for something up front (in this case, the shipping costs), it's much easier to get them to buy something else from you.

Pros

o   Moves a much higher volume of books and gets your message in the hands of more people (especially compared to the Traditional Launch)

o   Brings in a large amount of customers directly to you or your business (you keep the customers contact info, payment method, etc.)

o   Allows you to control the entire buying experience with your book, meaning better tracking, more leads, and the ability to upsell other products/services

Instead of Amazon or Kindle gaining a customer, in the Free-Plus Shipping Launch, customers are coming directly to you via your site. This means you get their information (email, address, etc.) and have more opportunity to build rapport with them, thus leading them to purchase your higher priced products (see "upsells" later in this chapter).

Cons

o   You must already have an existing website (or the time, ability, and/or money to build one).

o   You must have a secure system in place for holding customer information and processing orders.

o   You need backend revenue (products or services) to cover the costs of the hard-copy books you are offering.

- o   You are responsible for the fulfillment of all book orders in a timely and responsible manner (unless you choose to work with a fulfillment center or a distributor).

- o   You must have knowledge of direct response marketing as the implementation of the strategy is very complex.

- o   You must advertise and know how to do so effectively.

- o   You must create a working "funnel" (definition in the first step, below) from scratch if you don't have one already.

As given in one of the points above, the Free-Plus Shipping Launch will not work unless you have a backend revenue (something to sell after the initial purchase: an upsell) to cover the costs of the hard-copy books and advertising.

If you choose your advertising venues carefully and build a high converting funnel, your backend revenue will more than cover your marketing and book fulfillment expenses.

OVERVIEW OF THE FREE-PLUS SHIPPING LAUNCH STRATEGY

Your goal is to bring buyers to your site and get them to "climb the ladder" of products, starting with a purchase of the least expensive and moving up and up ("upselling") to your most expensive product. Your free, hard-copy book is the lure you use to entice buyers (1) to your site, (2) onto your subscriber list, and (3) onto your ladder of products because the free book is the first rung of the ladder.

The Free-Plus Shipping Launch method is a bit of a gamble, and that's why I only recommend it for the advanced. As I mentioned before, you have to have the backend revenue to cover all of your costs (advertising, fulfillment, etc). Otherwise, you are at risk for losing money on your books, especially in the short term.

The simple equation is this:

If your LTV (Lifetime Value) of a customer is greater than your CTAC (Cost To Acquire A Customer) + COGS (Cost Of Goods Sold), you have a profitable, working funnel.

$$LTV > CTAC + COGS = \$\$\$$$

The danger, and what scares away most people from this model, is that you likely won't know these numbers until you start your testing. . . meaning you won't know if it will be profitable or not until you try it.

UPSELLING THE CUSTOMER AND THE VALUE LADDER

With the Free-Plus Shipping method, getting the customer to purchase your other products is the end goal and the main reason for marketing the book this way.

But, you want to make sure to upsell them in the right order.

Let's say you have three products: a book, a course, and a "do it for you" product. Each time you upsell someone, the customer should get a higher valued, more in-depth, and more expensive product. You wouldn't want to offer them a course first (more expensive) and a free book second. You want to place the customer in a trajectory of investing in increasingly expensive products or services.

That's where The Value Ladder comes into play.

To understand the true meaning of a book funnel and upselling, you must first understand The Value Ladder.

There are three levels on the "Value Ladder":

1. *Teach them how to do it.* For this level, think instruction manual (or in your case, your book). This is the cheapest product in the value ladder. This is the most scaleable and also requires the least amount of delivery from you/your business. Your book has the information, but they're going to have to find the sections they need and put them into action.

2. *Show them how to do it.* This is a how-to video training, a course, or a more expensive product. You cover almost exactly the same information as the first level but with more detail.

3. *Do it for them.* Instead of telling or showing the customer how to do something, they pay the premium, and you do it for them. This can maximize the value of your customers but requires a lot more resources on your part, so plan accordingly. As an alternative to a "done-for-you" service, this could also be a conference, retreat, or higher priced mastermind.

Understand, that as you learn about creating a book funnel, each step or page of the funnel will be a rung in the value ladder. Each product offered in your funnel will add more value to the customer while simultaneously going up in price.

My friend, Russell Brunson was one of the pioneers of this method, selling twenty-two thousand copies of his book, *DotcomSecrets*, before it was even released!

By using a book funnel, like the one I'm about to explain, Russell was able to bring in hundreds of thousands of dollars for his business.

IMPLEMENTATION PLAN

Step 1: Create your funnel.
First, you'll want to build your book funnel, which will provide value to customers no matter what level of product they are willing to buy and will identify your top end buyers that can afford your most expensive products.

A book funnel is basically a way to move people through the sales process by offering them more and more expensive products as they navigate through your website:

1. A lot of people (traffic) enter as potential customers are interested in your product.

2. Some of those people continue through your funnel and buy your front end, cheaper product. This should be the first thing they see as as they begin navigating through your website.

3. Even fewer people will continue on through your funnel and buy your average priced product, which is something that is not too expensive, but not very cheap.

4. The people that want even more from you will then continue on through the end of the funnel where your top notch, most expensive product is housed.

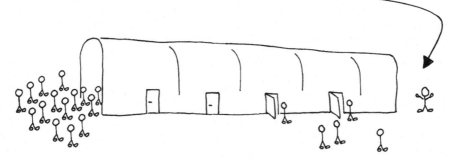

Remember, as each product builds through the funnel, it needs to add more and more value to the customers going through it.

Your funnel will consist of four main pages on your website:

1. *Free + Shipping home page*
   This is your main page where you attract customers, and they begin going through the funnel, by first deciding to take you up on your free book offer.

2. *Upsell #1 page*
   Your medium sized product, that adds more value than your book. This could be a speech, webinar, or online summit.

3. *Upsell #2 page*
   Your high end top level product, which is commonly a course of some kind.

4. *Thank You page*

   This is where you will thank the customers for the products they have bought and tell them what will happen next in the delivery of their products.

Step 2: Begin driving traffic.

Next, you'll want to test different pricing and advertising methods. These advertising methods will be a combination of everything mentioned in the previous launch methods, especially focusing on new marketing strategies rather than traditional marketing.

The main difference here is, you will be sending the traffic to your website and book funnel instead of to sites like Amazon.

Because you are responsible for sending traffic, it is also important to find paid traffic sources, such as Facebook or Google Adwords. By spending money on those traffic sources, you will be able to increase the amount of traffic to your site, leading into step three.

Step 3: Test, tweak, and improve.

Over the course of your launch, it is up to you to monitor which advertisements are working and which ones are not. You will be able to tell which direct marketing strategies are working, how many people are going through your funnel, and how many customers are buying and when.

Don't be afraid to pivot in your marketing strategies. Experiment with what you use, find what is working best, and concentrate on applying your energy to the marketing strategies that are working best.

Before finishing up with our last marketing strategy, I want to remind you one final time to not get discouraged if you found this method or The Traditional Price Strategy overwhelming.

Both of these methods are written for a specific group of people, and it's okay if that's not you. If it is, I'm sure you learned something valuable.

Now that you've learned about the four strategies and have chosen the one that best fits your situation and needs, in the next chapter, we will revisit marketing, one final time, to address reviews, and how to get them for your book.

We've all read reviews—whether for a movie, a smartphone, or a pair of socks. We've all depended on them. We've all written one too at sometime in our lives. So it will come as no surprise that you must have a lot of positive reviews to blast your book beyond the Earth's exosphere and into the glorious ethers of the best-selling superstars.

Chapter 21

THE BIG ASK

It's time to get reviews for your book.

When I think about my own significant experiences with reviews, the first thing that comes to mind is buying shoes online. I found sneakers I really liked, but they were made by a company I'd never bought from before. So, I found myself wondering, "Will they match my standard shoes size? What if they look great in the photos, but in reality, they are uncomfortable and take weeks to break in?"

Where did I go for answers? Customer reviews.

Expensive but worth it. Very well-made.
Half size small, but totally awesome.
Look great in pics but material seems cheap.

If I'm really serious about buying the shoes, I read several of the reviews and weigh other buyers' pros and cons to help me make my final decision. I have been on the fence about an online purchase, and enough "totally worth it" type reviews have convinced me to go through with the purchase.

Reviews do the exact same thing for your book. They validate your book for potential customers through previous readers' honest opinions. They prompt the potential reader that your book is worth the buy.

REQUESTING REVIEWS

This is what all that stealth marketing you'll be trickling out to your following over the course of the ninety days will be leading to—the BIG ASK. You'll have been following the give, give, involve, and give so much that when you reach this point, your followers will jump right in during this time when you need them most.

Because reviews are so vital to your success, I have made asking for reviews a simple process for you to follow. Below, I present the review request process in simple steps to make it as quick and painless as possible. I am even including some "dos and don'ts" to help you along the way.

Asking for reviews should happen in four places: (1) your email list (if you have one), (2) your launch team, (3) on social media, and (4) directly to supporters of the book.

Whether your email list was made yesterday and has eight people on it or you've been growing it for years, you need to ask those people to write you reviews. Every review counts.

And as I've said time and time again, it doesn't have to be via your social media that you leverage the success of your book. Use email. Use in-person interactions. Call friends, family members, colleagues, even neighbors on the phone to ask.

Review Push Step 1
When—Five days before your launch
What—

- Personally reach out to everyone who showed engagement, interest, and support in regard to your book journey and give them a free PDF version of your book as a thank you.

- You may use email, Facebook, Twitter, Snapchat, etc.

- Ask them not to share the PDF with others because your book hasn't been released yet.

- It is *especially* important to personally reach out to all the people who commented on or "liked" your stealth social media marketing messages. This is where you are going to get the most reviews because these people were already emotionally invested in your success and took the time to "like" and/or comment on a post.

Review Push Step 2

When—The moment your book is live in the Amazon store
What—

○ In this message, ask people to write reviews of your book and include a direct link.

○ Tell them your review goal: to receive [*number*] reviews by [*date*].

○ Tell them why you need the reviews: (1) you need the feedback to learn what worked and what didn't in your book, and (2) Amazon rewards books with lots of reviews by promoting those books on the site and beyond.

○ Also, include a PDF version of your book again.

Review Push Step 3

When—The first day of your launch
What—

○ Reach out again to the people you contacted in step one and two who have not written a review yet.

○ Ask them again to write you a review and include a direct link.

○ Tell them your review goal: to receive [*number*] reviews by [*date*].

○ Explain again why you need the reviews, but don't use the exact words you used previously.

THE BIG ASK USING AUTORESPONDERS

Autoresponders are emails that are automatically sent to people within your list, generating a set response to them.

When customers opt in to your subscribers list (via a link in your ebook, for example), they should automatically receive an email from you welcoming and thanking them. When you do this, you are also setting the stage for continued communication with the buyer.

Scheduling autoresponders can yield huge results in terms of boosting your review count, especially if you systematically send out the appropriate emails at the right time.

Once you have at least a few people on your email list, you should strategically send emails, written to trigger the people on your list to take action. Below, you'll find email templates you can modify to fit your needs.

What happens if you have a greater reach with your social network than you do with your email list? That's what's great about the email templates below. You can just change a few words around (make them seem more like a post instead of an email), and you are still going to prompt people to take action.

Through rigorous testing, I've figured out what email templates convert best to action (getting a review), as well as the best way to optimize the timing of the emails.

Here are the steps in my approach to motivate people who have bought my book and opted in to take the next step and write a review for the book too. I still use this process when doing a review push for my newest books.

Part 1—Initial Email
When: Set it up to automatically send immediately upon person's opting in.

What: Set up the following email as an autoresponder to be sent out as a "thank you" to anyone that has downloaded the book and signed up for the opt-in and/or free giveaway.

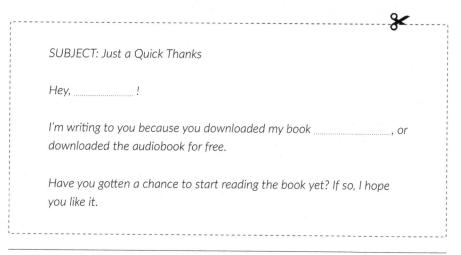

SUBJECT: Just a Quick Thanks

Hey, ... !

I'm writing to you because you downloaded my book ...., or downloaded the audiobook for free.

Have you gotten a chance to start reading the book yet? If so, I hope you like it.

I'm sending this email out to say THANK YOU for your support.

Since launching the book, ... people have downloaded it, and it is currently ranked ....

This book is a HUGE win for me so far, and YOU are making it successful!

Hit "reply" to this email and let me know what you think of the book. I can't wait to hear how .... is changing your life!

Talk soon!

P.S. Please reply sometime today. I'd love to hear your feedback ASAP!

Part 2—Follow Up for Feedback Email

When: Set it up to automatically send two days after the initial "thank you" email.

What: Follow up with the first email, and do a soft push for a review.

SUBJECT: Thanks for the Feedback!

Hey, ... !

Just following up on the email I sent on ....

As you know if you saw that email, my new book just launched, and it's really starting to be a success!

I was floored at how many of you responded to my last email and told me how much you liked the book.

Would you mind copying and pasting what you emailed and leave it as a review on Amazon?

That would be a HUGE help.

Click here to leave a quick review.

My goal is to get _____ reviews by the end of the week, and, as I write this email, I'm sitting at _____.

The review doesn't have to be more than 2 sentences, and you can always go back and change it later.

Can you take 2 seconds right now to leave a review?

I just need you to leave a review by _____, so we can hit our goal of _____ reviews.

Thanks SO MUCH for your support!

Click here to leave a review.

Part 3—Thank You

When—One week after the first day of your launch

What—The last thing you want to do is send out a quick email thanking everyone for their support. Don't forget to include the final stats for your book in this email.

SUBJECT: This really means a lot . . .

First off, BIG thanks to everyone who took the time to leave me a review on Amazon!

It's because of the hundreds of you that responded to my cry for help that I reached the top.

Wanna know exactly how successful _____ really was?

Good news!!

I've got the stats here.

During the final minutes of my launch week, a total of............people downloaded my book, and it is currently ranked............!

That's insane!

I couldn't have done it without your help.
You guys are the best!

P.S. If you haven't had the chance to read and review the book, that's okay. I'd still LOVE to read your feedback. Click here to leave a review.

The Dos

The Don'ts

The Dos	The Don'ts
Use the templates I made for you. I use it when I launch books, so I know it works.	Don't be afraid. In general, people want to help you, so just ask.
Provide people with a link to your book and/or a free PDF.	Don't beg. People will either leave a review or they won't. I usually don't ask more than twice.
Ask the people that gave you input on your title and cover for a review first.	Don't get upset when people don't leave you a review.
Keep track of who left you a reivew, how you contacted them, and the book they reviewed. This will help you out later.	Don't forget to thank the people that left you a review.
Reach out to everyone through a personal message with their name. It's okay to copy and paste the same message, just change who it is addressed to.	Don't set an unrealistic goal for the number of reviews you want. Only hope for the amount of reviews that makes sense for the size of your following.

DONE

That's basically all there is to it!

Like I said before, there is a wrong and a right way to ask for reviews. You have to give value to receive it. Remember Gary Vaynerchuck's Jab, Jab, Jab, Right Hook philosophy? Give, give, involve, give some more— and then ask. It's imperative that you share your author-hero's journey with them over the course of a few months, so that when you finally ask them to help you out and write a review, they are more than happy to do so.

Giving away some of your books and products, as I suggested, is just another element in that same philosophy—so don't be stingy with your product. A single review is going to help you more in the long run than the money you will receive from a book purchase.

Never underestimate the power your list can have, even if it's small. Because of the reviews I gained from my email list, my book is twice as credible as it was before.

As of right now, my book is sitting at 550 reviews and counting.

With these clear steps to follow in your big review push, you'll land many amazing reviews too.

We've now reached the end of the SPS 90-Day Way, and to close, I want to share with you my "why" behind this book and behind why I'm so passionate about teaching this information.

In the first chapter, I gave my big goal for *Published.*—I want you to honestly believe you can write a book to achieve your dreams. Now I want you to know why I'm so passionate about teaching this information and giving the gift of writing a book to as many people as possible.

Chapter 22

MAKE HIM PROUD

In the fall of 2014, I went on a three-day cruise to the Bahamas to celebrate the success of the top achievers in my former company.

We hung out on the beach during the day, playing games and enjoying the clean air and water. At night we had fun too. . .dancing, having dinner, even talking about our dreams and goals for the coming year. It was a special time for this small group of high achievers, a time of great energy and high hopes.

Kendall, one of the younger managers, was a friend and, in a way, he almost seemed like a younger brother to me.

One night at dinner, when we all were sharing our five-year goals, Kendall confided in me that he wanted to help more people and become a stronger leader in the company. He also talked about his passion project, "The Driven Vision," helping young twenty something's create more opportunity for themselves and make better decisions.

He even shared his sales goal: $500K in the coming year (meaning more jobs created and young people helped). As I said, it was a bonding, hope-filled experience.

The night after this dinner conversation my world was turned upside down. It was totally unexpected, and it changed my life forever.

It was the final night of the celebration cruise. My friends and I were up on the ship, having fun, and planning for our futures. Time flew. I had really missed being around such great people and inspiring young business leaders.

The night was just coming to an end when everything quickly took a turn for the worse.

Unexpectedly, Kendall was swept over the railing on the upper deck.

He fell two stories.

"Kendall, are you okay?!" I yelled.

I fully expected him to get up and laugh it off.

Then, a chilling realization hit me—he wasn't moving.

"Help! Help! Somebody get some help!"

I rushed down to where he lay, and I was the first person to reach him.

Kendall wasn't responding. Nothing I was doing was waking him, and he was still unconscious. Minutes passed as a crowd gathered around, staring, unsure of what to do. I felt helpless.

A pit in my stomach arose as I realized there was nothing I could do. All I could do was stay with him and pray as hard as I could.

Someone had called the paramedics several minutes earlier, but none had shown up yet.

"Where are the paramedics? Why are they taking so long to get to us?" I thought to myself. Everyone around me was wondering the same thing.

It was as if time stood still while Kendall's life hung in the balance.

I felt powerless. Moments previously we'd been a confident, secure group of entrepreneurs and friends reminiscing about the past and talking about the future. Now we were all helpless.

The paramedics finally arrived and took Kendall into their care.

As I was waiting outside Kendall's medical room, the helpless feeling began to overcome me. Just the previous night, Kendall had been sharing with me his five-year plan. Now he was laid up in a bed, and it wasn't looking good.

We hurried back into port. As soon as possible, Kendall was rushed to a hospital.

He didn't make it. Kendall died on the way to the hospital. He was 20 years old.

I was an emotional wreck. I replayed the scenario over and over in my mind. "What could I have done differently to save Kendall's life?"

I experienced guilt, grief, and I was totally shaken. My heart broke for his family as they found out their only son had passed away.

To make matters even worse, even more heart-wrenching—an hour later I received news that my grandmother, "Nanny," had also passed away while I was on the cruise.

As you can imagine, I'd never had anything like that happen to me before, and I didn't know how to handle it.

FINDING THE POSITIVE

A week after Kendall passed away, I got the chance to talk with his dad. He told me how Kendall was his only son, the carrier of the family name, and that he was too old to have any more children.

He went on to confide in me that the only positive, the only good that could possibly come from the abrupt death of his only son was if others' lives can somehow benefit from it.

He knew that if others' lives could change for the better because of this incident, it would help to ease some of the pain.

I was amazed at the courage and selflessness of Kendall's dad and his family during this difficult time. Their focus on others, even in a time of duress, shows exactly why Kendall was such a great man and a great leader.

A WAKE-UP CALL

This all happened during a tough time in my life. I'd just dropped out of college and my business (my only source of income) was struggling—both of which made me feel very jaded and focused on the wrong things.

I was concentrated on money, fame, and making a name for myself, even at the expense of all the things that really mattered. At the same time my friend—a great person with such integrity and care for others—unexpectedly died before my eyes.

Kendall's father's words—*if only others' lives can somehow benefit from Kendall's death*—touched me deeply.

Those words, and Kendall's tragic, accidental death brought me to a place where I was forced to ask myself some tough questions—

Does what I am doing really matter?
Am I making a difference?
Am I making the world a better place?
If I were to die tomorrow, would I be happy with the life I've lived?

From these, I moved on to even more pressing questions—

How can I make a difference?
How can I make Kendall proud?
How can I make the world a better place?
How can I help accomplish his goals and dreams that he'll never be able to accomplish?

I realized that I no longer believed that money equalled success. I was forced to acknowledge my highly practical, objective take on the world and then soften it, allowing my emotions, feelings, and care for others to return to my everyday life.

I was forced to carefully consider the new business I'd started, Self-Publishing School—

> *Through this business, will I make a difference in the world?*
> *Will SPS make the world a better place?*
> *Would Kendall be proud of it?*

After some careful thinking, I concluded—YES. Yes to all of the above. Yes to finding some kind of benefit, some little piece of positivity from my dear friend's passing. Yes to making Kendall proud.

Why "yes"?

So many people, both SPS students and readers of my books, regularly contact me in emails, Facebook messages, client calls, and even hand-written letters to tell me how they've followed my approach, written and published their first books, and how life-changing and empowering the whole experience was for them.

For these first-time writers, books are tools for broadcasting their messages, their hearts, their lives, their skills, their causes for sadness and reasons for joy—and yes, this matters. It is making our world a better place.

MY ROCKEFELLER MOMENT

A few months later, I found myself watching the miniseries, *The Men Who Built America*.

In one scene, John D. Rockefeller scheduled a very important business meeting with Cornelius Vanderbilt. The meeting required Rockefeller to take a train up to see Vanderbilt in person.

Before catching the train, Rockefeller felt compelled to visit his church to pray. Then, on the way to the train station from the church, his carriage broke down. The pit stop at his church, plus the broken down carriage, caused him to miss his train and reschedule the most important meeting of his life.

At the time, it was a setback and a frustrating event.

Then, a week later, Rockefeller learned some startling news. The train he missed ended up derailing and falling off of a bridge en route, killing everyone on board. As you can imagine, this greatly impacted Rockefeller's life, much like Kendall's passing did for me.

Decades later, Rockefeller reflected on this event and called it his "defining moment." It was that time in his life that made him realize he was on this earth for a reason. It was God that called him to the church, causing him to miss his train. And he was still alive because God had a bigger plan for him to carry out.

Hearing this story, I related—not in a self-serving, egotistical way—but from my experience with Kendall's death.

Kendall's abrupt passing was by far the largest defining moment in my life. It was a moment that changed everything. It gave my life a purpose, a reason, a drive—to make this world a better place, beyond myself. It's my "why," and it drives me every single day to achieve my potential and make the world a better place.

YOUR TURN

I share all this to issue you a challenge—

> *Ask yourself some tough questions:*
> *— Does what you are doing right now really matter?*
> *— Are you making this world a better place?*
> *— If you were to die tomorrow, would you be happy with what you've done so far, with the life you've lived?*

Take some time and ask yourself these tough questions. Take your time and really consider them.

If the answer is no, then decide to make some changes. Decide to live a life that matters.

What could that look like?

Maybe, like a first-time writer recently shared with me, you will quit your job and start an art studio.

Maybe you'll decide to use all those vacation days you've accrued in one go, and you'll spend six weeks exploring British Columbia in a RV.

Maybe you'll go back to school and study what you really want.

Maybe you'll stop chasing money.

Maybe you'll train for a marathon with your senior-citizen mother.

Maybe you'll write that book that's been in your head all these years.

There's so much more behind what you are doing. You have the potential to really change the world if you cut the crap and focus on what really matters.

I don't want it to take a life altering event (like it did for me) for you to make those changes.

A LEGACY. YOUR LEGACY.

Following my advice and encouragement, my friend Kendall had just finished writing a book, *Mastering a Career Fair*, before he died, but he never got to publish it.

Along with the help of my peers, we made sure that it was published, so his legacy can live on forever.

But for me, that's not enough.

It's become my life mission to share this particular writing process, the SPS 90-Day Way, with as many people as possible because I know you have a book inside you that you need to share with the world. I know how life-changing and empowering writing that book will be, both for you and for your readers.

Everyday I wear a bracelet saying, "Make Him Proud," as a constant reminder that pushes me to never stop living the life Kendall would have wanted for me.

It's my mission to help you leave your mark on the world as I am leaving mine. We aren't guaranteed tomorrow, so we need to live today.

What are you doing to leave your legacy behind?

THROUGH THE WARDROBE AND INTO NARNIA

Choose unlimited possibilities.

That's the motto, the driving force, the passion I want to impart to you in this book.

It's contagious.

Going through the writing, marketing, and publishing process in just ninety days is no small feat. You have to choose those unlimited possibilities if you want to pull it off, especially when you have a full-time job, two side jobs, and three kids. That's what Omer Redden, author of *Give and Grow Rich*, was balancing when he bought into the motto and started living it. Here's Omer's take on it:

Not only did I write a bestseller utilizing the information from this book and from their paid program, now, I have a home business. And I have the privilege of working with/for SPS. Here's how it happened, in three sentences:

At the end of 2014, I took a program from Michael Hyatt called, "Best Year Ever," and, as a result, I wrote out three HUGE goals for the year. I wanted to publish a bestseller, get out of my dead-end job, and start working from home. Because of SPS and because I chose "unlimited possibilities," I've been able to hit all three goals.

Here's the crazy thing—you can do the same thing. You can achieve your dreams, you can reach your goals, you can live the life you want, and you can leave a legacy.

You'll have to make some sacrifices. You'll have to develop a new mindset. And you'll even become an author along the way, sharing that distinction with Kendall, Omer, and me, three ordinary people who found a way to create more value in the world by sharing knowledge with others, shaped by our unique life experiences.

At the surface, writing a book can be a financially and personally worthwhile endeavor. However, there is so much more to it than that, if you let it be.

Choose unlimited possibilities.

Chapter 23

CHOOSE UNLIMITED POSSIBILITES

It's Your Time To Publish.

With the SPS 90-Day Way, you have a zero percent chance of your book being a flop.

If Michael Unks, a pharmacist from South Carolina, can write multiple best-selling books in under six months, so can you.

If Carly Danielle can channel her outrage and anxiety about her sister and father's cancer diagnoses into a best-selling book, so can you.

If Shelia Merkel and Ben Schwipps can turn the story behind Ben's tragic suicide attempt into a best-selling book to help others, so can you.

Hundreds of people have found success with these methods: Lindy Mayberry Sellers, Olivia Gamber, R.E. Vance, Omer Redden, Samantha Roose—the list of first-time writers who wrote best-selling books and changed their lives for the better goes on and on. Let's put your name on that list too.

You may have some late nights or early mornings. You may miss a few of your favorite TV shows, but know the possibilities that will arise from becoming an author will outweigh the small things you may temporarily give up.

WHY I WROTE THIS BOOK

I wrote this book because I want to share the process of becoming an author with everyone and anyone that will listen. I want you to make a difference in your life and the world around you by writing a book and sharing the knowledge you already possess.

I want to give you the tools to gain the freedom to do whatever you want with your life when you want to do it. The tools in this book allow you to do just that.

I want to make it easier on you to make your dreams a reality.

As you know, before you can do any of those things, however, you have to believe in yourself and know you can write a book.

I know you can do it. All you have to do is follow the SPS 90-Day Way that I presented to you in this book. This is the same approach that has already helped so many people all around the world become authors.

The key is to take action; take the first step and begin the process of writing. Make the commitment to yourself. Decide today that you *will* write a book.

If I can go from a college dropout and a C-level English student to a best-selling author, so can you.

You picked up this book for a reason. It sparked your interest because you have something to share, a story to tell. Whatever your motivation is, write your book and make your lasting impression on the world.

The door is open.

The decision to enter is yours.

SELF-PUBLISHING SCHOOL: OUR BIGGER MISSION

Self-Publishing School is how I am fulfilling some of Kendall's dreams and making the world a better place. Everything I do, I do to make him proud, to carry out his legacy, to help others, and to make the world a better place.

I created Self-Publishing School to offer people even greater support in writing their books.

At SPS, our mission is to enable people to choose *unlimited possibilities*.

If you know you want to write a book and think you might want the extra support SPS can give, I encourage you to check out Self-Publishing School. I promise it will be the best investment you ever make in yourself.

If you're interested in the program, I've created a four-video training series that will teach you even more about writing and launching your first book. It'll also give you further information on SPS.

Check out the video training program here: http://self-publishingschool.com/free

Regardless of whether or not you want to join us at Self-Publishing School, I want to hear your success stories!

I hope you will send me a note when you publish your book, telling me how you are doing and how your life has changed as a result of becoming an author.

You can reach me at chandler@self-publishingschool.com.

Here's to you becoming an author! And here's to your first book being *Published*.

Chandler Bolt

- BONUS -

In case you want a more in depth, step-by-step look at the writing, launching, and marketing process, I am going to give you a free audiobook download of my ebooks, How To NOT SUCK At Writing Your First Book and Book Launch. Plus a link to sign up for my exclusive Mastermind Community for just $1!

How to NOT Suck At Writing Your First Book Link:
http://self-publishingschool.com/how-to-not-suck-at-writing/
free-writing-audiobook/

Book Launch Link:
http://self-publishingschool.com/freeaudiobook

Mastermind Community:
http://self-publishingschool.com/s/mastermind-community/

URGENT PLEA!

Thank You For Reading My Book!

I really appreciate all of your feedback, and
I love hearing what you have to say.

I need your input to make the next version of this book and
my future books better.

Please leave me a helpful review on Amazon letting me
know what you thought of the book.

Thanks so much!!

~ Chandler Bolt

Made in the USA
Columbia, SC
12 April 2018